OBJECTS AND FURNITURE DESIGN

EILEEN GRAY

By Architects

© of the edition: 2020 Polígrafa
www.poligrafa.com

© of the texts, translations, and photographs: the authors

Research and texts: Sandra Dachs, Patricia de Muga, Laura García Hintze and Nuria Jorge
Design of the series: mot_studio

ISBN: 978-84-343-1496-2

Available in the USA and Canada through D.A.P./Distributed Art Publishers
155 Sixth Avenue, 2nd Floor, New York, N.Y. 10013
Tel. (212) 627-1999 Fax: (212) 627-9484

Back cover: From Eileen Gray and Jean Badovici, "De l'éclectisme au doute", L'Architecture Vivante, fall-winter 1929.

OBJECTS AND FURNITURE DESIGN

EILEEN GRAY

Introduction by Carmen Espegel

Edited by Sandra Dachs, Patricia de Muga,
Laura García Hintze and Nuria Jorge

Ediciones Polígrafa

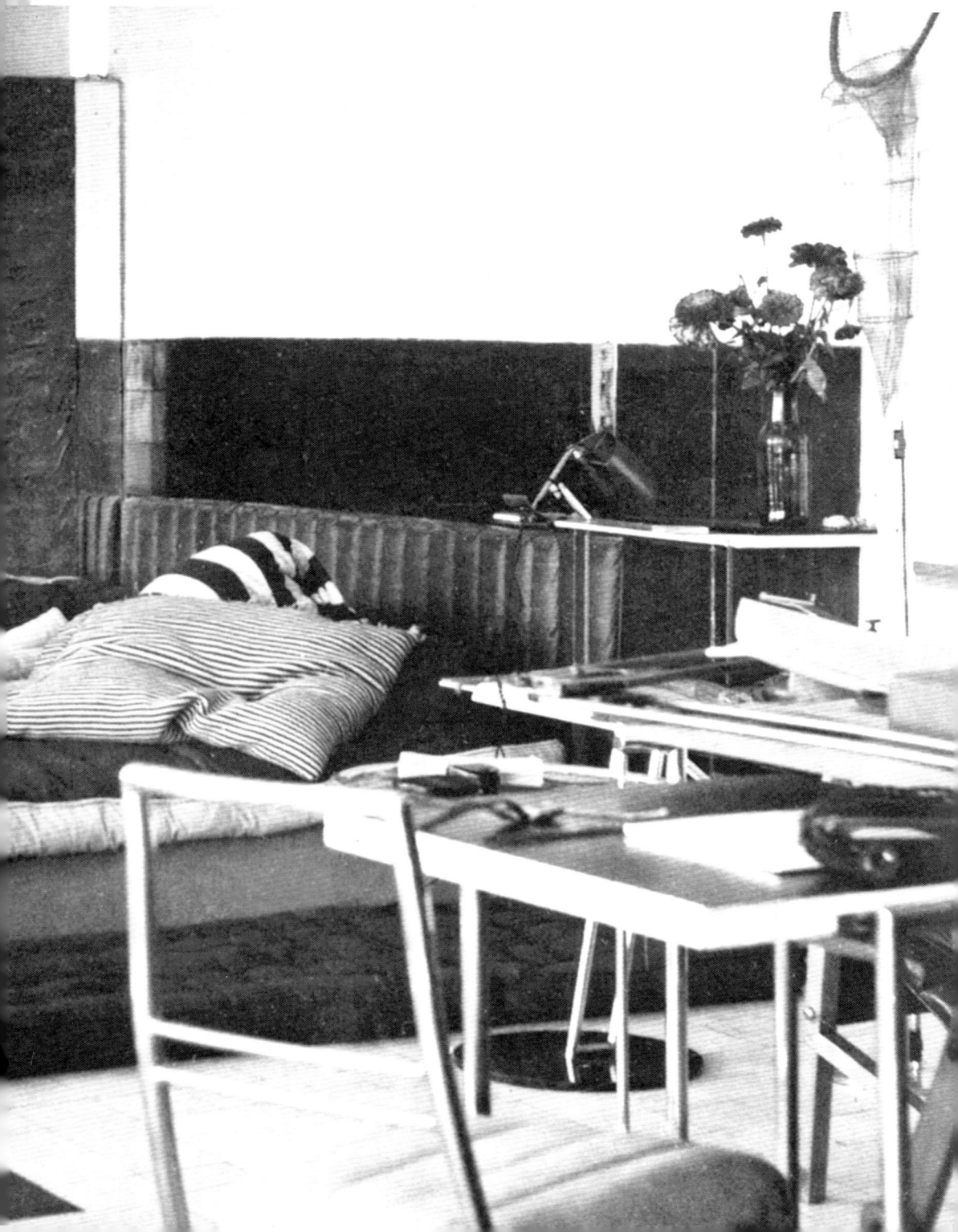

LIST OF CONTENTS

INTRODUCTION
MODERN CONSTELLATION

CARMEN ESPEGEL

"However, this intellectual coldness we have arrived at, and which interprets only too well the harsh laws of modern machinism, can only be a temporary phenomenon. We must once again find the human being in the plastic outward show, the human will behind the material outward show, and the pathetic nature of this modern life that was formerly seen merely as a kind of translation of the language of algebra."[1]

Eileen Gray

Intensity. That perhaps is the best word to describe the impression made by the work of the Anglo-Irish designer and architect Eileen Gray. To this day, her lyrical works filled with a sense of vitality continue to express a clear and vigorous voice in a world of design that the uninitiated might often perceive as inward-looking and, in its drift towards art, increasingly remote from the ordinary user. This spiritual energy, this vital force, might explain why it is that Gray's pieces have managed to combine supreme aesthetic quality with a transcendence—though late in coming—that makes them a case apart. Current sales catalogues of her pieces give an idea of the magnitude and wealth of her work.

During the 1920s and 1930s, Gray's furniture, interior designs and works of architecture were published in leading journals such as *L'Architecture Vivante*, *L'Architecture d'Aujourd'hui*, *Der Baumeister*, *Les Cahiers d'Art*, *L'Arredamento Moderno*, *Wendingen*, *Vogue* and *Harper's Bazaar*. In the 1940s and 1950s, however, they virtually disappeared from the pages of publications focused on modernity. It was not until 1968 that Joseph Rykwert took up Gray's cause, describing her as a "pioneer of design." Later, the screen she had ironically entitled "Le Destin" sold for $36,000 at the famous auction of furnishings from the private collection of the couturier and patron of the arts Jacques

1. Dialogue "De l'éclectisme au doute", *L'Architecture Vivante*, fall-winter 1929.

Doucet, held at the Hôtel Drouot in Paris. The significant value of the sale drew attention to Gray, and her name once again appeared in the press, though journalists at the time were little concerned with architectural theories, leading to a certain amount of confusion regarding the merit and quality of her creations.

An uncompromising woman, Gray always designed for herself, in other words, for a specific person. Her many works (150 designs and 45 architectural and interior renovation projects, of which only nine were constructed) drew unqualified admiration from the most demanding critics, who recognized in her output an ethical and aesthetic experiment of unwavering rigor. She was independent of mind, reserved and solitary, and had no wish to join any of the groups of the day, though she maintained links with the radical avant-garde movements. Her long career, extending over 70 years of intellectual production, enabled her to observe how her work served as a nexus between the modern pioneers and their revisionist critics.

NON-CONFORMIST

Born in Ireland into a distinguished family, Gray spent her childhood partly in the country of her birth and partly in London, a city that allowed her to direct her education towards art and drawing. She was able, nevertheless, to escape straitlaced Victorian Britain by emigrating to Paris in 1902, where she continued her studies in graphic art and painting. The capital of Cubism, Art Deco and Sergey Diaghilev's Ballets Russes, which so influenced Gray's work due to the harmony they established between the body, movement and furnishings, and the self-same city where Erik Satie earned a meager living as a cabaret musician, this Paris in upheaval would be Gray's adopted home until her death in 1976.

Gray learned the art of lacquer ware in London but became expert in it by studying with Seizo Sougawara, a Japanese master living in Paris. Gray improved her technique by experimenting with metal and mother-of-pearl inlays, and by expanding the range of colors beyond the traditional hues of black, vermillion, and chestnut, to the extent that she succeeded in achieving deep blues and greens.

In her pieces, she strove to bring opposites together in an attempt to create works that fused modernity and tradition, functionalism and spirituality, abstraction and figuration. It is perhaps because of this that "Le Destin", which she put her signature to 1913, encapsulates this path that would lead Gray to create her most markedly modern pieces. This screen in four panels lacquered in red combines a reverse side decorated with sinuous abstract lines with an allegorical scene on the front that depicts two young male nudes, one of them carrying an old man wrapped in a cloak. The discord between these two styles heralded the syncretism of her future designs. In 1918, she started work on her first comprehensive interior design project, which she undertook in several phases, incorporating lacquer work, textiles and furniture into the apartment on Rue de Lota belonging to Madame Mathieu-Lévy, the second owner of the Suzanne Talbot fashion salon. An eccentric atmosphere of Oriental sensuality was in vogue at the time she began this renovation work, yet Eileen Gray was able to distance herself from it by devising a unified, functional and abstract proposal that was essentially modern yet evidently contained a certain respect for the old. In her design, she contrasted sumptuous furnishings with panels decorated with rhythmical waves, a large collection of ancient art, and, in her final intervention in 1924, a vestibule lined with 450 blocks lacquered in black. The overall effect of these contrasts was to create a cohesive whole.

Like Pierre Chareau and Francis Jourdain, Eileen Gray opened her own showroom to sell her works, the Galerie Jean Désert at number 217 on Rue du Faubourg Saint-Honoré. Curiously enough, the most popular items sold by the shop, which remained in business between 1922 and 1930, were the rugs she designed and had made by hand by a group of rug weavers supervised by her friend Evelyn Wyld. During these crucial years, this shop witnessed the artist's gradual transition from a decorative

aesthetic to modern machinist splendor. Gray seems to have been wholly familiar with each material she employed in her objects, its raison-d'être, its limitations and its peculiarities, be it steel, sycamore or celluloid. A team of craftsmen and women helped her to perfect each piece by means of successive alterations until she arrived at the finished object. Each design thus achieved was far removed from the notion of a prototype and instead much closer to the concept of a model. Capable of holding many ideas at once in her mind, she had the ability to combine intellectual rigor with the beauty of fine craftsmanship. For her early pieces, which were in keeping with Art Deco, she chose extremely sensual, luxurious, sumptuous materials. Later, however, she tended towards the industrial austerity of modern materials. She also selected the appropriate technique for each object or situation in order to satisfy the desire for comfort or to create visual appeal.

The mysterious and abstract Monte-Carlo Bedroom-Boudoir, shown at the Salon des Artistes Décorateurs in 1923, heralded the single spaces she would divide into zones by means of furnishings. This bedroom was an eclectic work that combined various different functions in a single, almost independent space brought to life by a breath of lyricism. The room's dimensions, transformations and multiple uses meant that it served as a kind of complex cell equipped for personal growth.

MODERN

It was not until 1926, however, that she ventured, self-taught, into architecture, taking a radical new direction by planning and building a villa at Roquebrune, her E.1027 house, Maison en bord de mer, in keeping with the style of the modern Avant-garde but employing a design that illustrates her constant critical thinking. She enunciated the shortcomings of the *machine à habiter* advocated by Le Corbusier by revealing that architecture usually arises in that space that goes beyond necessity, in order to attain inspiration. In this small yet infinite house, human existence reverberates out towards the phenomenological event. The primary functions are concealed, disclosing previously unknown new uses, turning the occupant into an actor engaged in a dialogue with a living, mercurial stage set that turns each useful element into an *objet d'art*, creating a place intended for human pleasure and delight.

Gray shows her mastery when combining two seemingly opposite principles of composition: *collage-objet trouvé* and symmetry. Firstly, in a continuous space she brings together elements that are initially mismatched but ultimately conjoined in a balanced whole of complementary parts. Similarly, the volumetric schemes used in Roquebrune, the syntactical rules of plastic composition, are based on moving a volume or surface off-center, breaking it up, linking it or folding it. However, her eclecticism is most clearly evident in a type of modernity rooted in English domesticity and the Mediterranean tradition. The rationalist functionality of the Anglo-American interior combined with the Mediterranean character of the naturalist relationship with the land, the use of open constructions and climate control, make her an unusual exponent of the Avant-garde.

In all her projects, the traditional divide between interior design and architecture is inconceivable, since a process of conversion takes place, turning the building into part of the furniture. Her holistic approach to architecture and everything related to it led her to integrate the various arts into a totality. Her wall coverings acquire a more solid appearance by incorporating, by way of macrostructures, the density of furniture. Likewise, the fixed and movable objects create a constant sense of variety in the space. Walls, windows, awnings, niches, screens, built-in features, drapes, screens, rugs and divans constitute an indissoluble multi-layered construction, a choreographic whole brimming with poetry. Gray's furniture designs do not belong to a specific style but are suited to their particular function, though this may fluctuate between a departure from and a dialectic with the everyday. Even the titles of her furnishings are both enigmatic and modern in tone: for a man who refuses to accept the established state of affairs, there is the "Nonconformist Chair"; for the traveler voyaging across the oceans, the "Transat" Chair; and for the racing car driver, the "Bibendum" Chair.

Gray would design a tapestry with the same passion as a home, producing drawings on various scales, from the geometrical concept to the smallest constructional detail. Everything was integrated in a single document with an extreme degree of abstraction, almost to the point of indecipherability, so much so that scholars have on occasion confused the design of a wardrobe front with that of a rug. In her following works, she continued her research. For Jean Badovici's small apartment on Rue de Chateaubriand in Paris, she set about taking the mechanist atmosphere, first found in Roquebrune, to the limit. In Tempe à Pailla, near the mountains of Castellar, she took the absence of sophistication in the interiors to extremes, presenting them as even more arid, clean, bare and austere than those she had designed for Badovici.

PRECURSOR

Though it was not Gray's intention, her works became the starting point for a critical revision of the Modern Movement, as her pieces drew together the various trends of the Avant-garde of the 1920s and breathed soul into strict rationalism, something that the third generation would embrace in the 1950s.

In restoring the world of the senses to scientific thinking, Eileen Gray was a pioneer, as she herself suggested in a conversation with Jean Badovici that was featured as part of the article on E.1027 published in the journal *L'Architecture Vivante*, which Badovici edited. When Badovici asked her if she was not afraid that the theoretical abstraction of modern architecture might not satisfy human spiritual and physical needs, Gray replied that the syncretism of the two concepts (science-abstraction and senses-spirituality) was inevitable. She went on to say that intellectual coldness was necessary to free modern architecture from any formal burden and thus allow it to take root and develop. But this period of transition, this "temporary phenomenon", was now over and it was essential to find the human being who would inhabit Architecture. In Gray's words, there was a need to return to "an emotionality purified by knowledge, enriched by the idea, and which does not exclude an understanding and appreciation of scientific achievements."

Thus, Gray's valuable body of work, closely linked to architecture and conceived in terms of construction elements, was created for the "modern man" who combines the twin qualities of supreme sensitivity and reason. Her somewhat utopian stance allowed her to research the human habitat with a view to improving it, as she demonstrated in her various projects following Roquebrune. These were concerned with minimal homes, collective buildings, and the holiday center, a response to the passing of a law in France in 1936 that established the right to a month's paid leave.

Few designers have expressed so much with so little. Her self-imposed obligation to restrict herself to the essential, to do away with any incidental embellishment, did not, however, set her on a path to sterile functionalism. On the contrary, there is something that gives these objects—which are, to a certain extent, conversation pieces—a secret magnetism, creating a shrine that keeps them alive in the memory. This body of work relies on a refined mastery of the craft of construction, on art as a vicarious continuation of life. In it, Eileen Gray displays a skill difficult to equal.

Eileen Gray's lacquerwork tools and materials.

LACQUER FURNITURE AND OBJECTS

Eileen Gray showed an early fascination with the elegant qualities of lacquerwork and went to Paris to continue her studies with the Japanese lacquer master Seizo Sugawara. Under his tutelage, she learned everything she needed to know about the ancient craft of lacquerwork. As a result of her determination to achieve perfection in the craft, she created extraordinary hues and colors, among them her prized blue color, which she was to use repeatedly, superseding the traditional tones of black, red and brown. She experimented with various materials such as gold leaf, mother-of-pearl, metal, sand and even smoking paper in order to give her works different textures and low-relief effects. If we look at her work as a whole, we see a process of change in the themes she chose for decorating large surfaces, passing from figurative forms to geometrical ones with a certain abstract symbolism inspired by Russian Constructivism and Kandinsky in particular. In 1913, she was invited to show her work in the Eighth Salon of the Société des Artistes Décorateurs. It was there that she attracted the attention of Jacques Doucet, a famed couturier and an important art collector of the day, who launched her career.

A page from the British edition of the August 1917 issue of *Vogue* magazine, showing two of the panels purchased by Jacques Doucet. Top centre: "La Voie Lactée". Bottom: "Le Destin".

AN ARTIST IN LACQUER

Some of Us Paint Miniatures, Weave Strange Tissues, or "Do Things With a Pen," But Miss Eileen Gray Chooses Lacquer As a Medium of Expression

What is the mystery which impels? What desire sways these strange figures? This door when completed—the illustration represents only a part of the design—will be more than usually interesting. Miss Gray who is a successful artist in "oils," fascinated by the difficulties of lacquer, now gives it her undivided attention

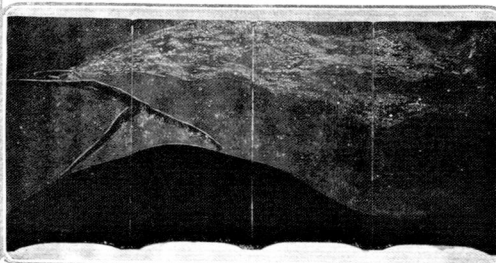

(Centre, above) This beautiful screen of blue lacquer is very simple but most effective in design. By what process of rubbing, by what mixture of resin and colour, by what subtle feeling for decorative line her effects are produced, only Miss Gray knows, but the results are here for all to wonder at; for all to covet

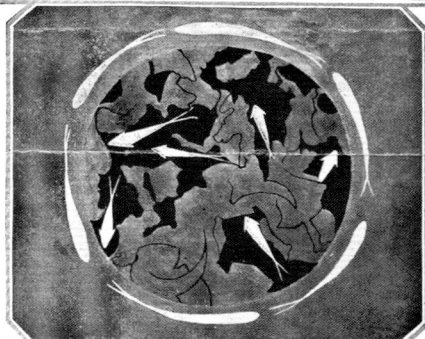

SOME of us paint miniatures. Some of us, as Kipling puts it, "do things with a pen." Some of us weave strange tissues on hand-looms. Suspecting ourselves of histrionic ability we aspire to the stage, or cherish secret hopes of one day figuring in politics. But not one of us—is there, indeed, one other?—has chosen, as has Miss Eileen Gray, lacquer as a medium of expression.

For years a successful artist in oils, it was in search of a new medium that Miss Gray opened, as it were, a lacquered gate and entered a new field. Her first production was a lacquered screen, and then, fascinated by the difficulties of the work, she made another; afterwards designing tables, chairs, and other objects which she executed in lacquer.

Artists saw her work and pronounced it good. Collectors saw it and added specimens of Miss Gray's lacquer to their collections. No less a person of taste than Doucet purchased the screen shown in the centre below. Very striking in colour is this screen, which is done in brilliant red lacquer. The nude figures are rendered in dark blue with just a suggestion of silver in the outline, which throws the figures slightly in relief, and the draped, mysterious figure is done in silver.

By what process of rubbing, by what mixture of resin and colour, by what subtle feeling for decorative line Miss Gray produces her effects, only Miss Gray knows; but the results are here for us all to wonder at, for us all to covet.

The difficulties of the work are great. Best adapted to lacquer are flat surfaces, which are carefully covered with cloth

Influenced by the modernists is Miss Gray's art, so they say. But is it not rather that she stands alone, unique, the champion of a singularly direct free method of expression, and for this she has chosen the strange medium of lacquer. This design for a table-top, which dimly suggests the zodiac, is palely illumined by a silver planet

(Left) There is something Japanese in the spirit of this sand-grey table-top, where white fishes dart about a black pool, in which float strange grey leaf forms. Best adapted to lacquer are flat surfaces carefully covered with cloth or silk before the resinous gum is applied, thus rendering the grain of the wood for ever invisible

or silk before the resinous gum is applied, thus rendering the grain of the wood for ever invisible. Then—but it is forbidden to write of the manner in which colour is mixed with the gum, which, by a process of rubbing and drying—and lacquer perversely dries best in a damp atmosphere—results in the mirror-like, flinty surface we know so well.

Miss Gray is an artist of rather an extraordinary sort, expressing herself sometimes with a terseness which is almost Japanese, as in the sand-grey table-top reproduced in the centre of this page, where white fishes dart about a black pool in which float strange grey leaf-forms. Again, as in the design for a door shown at the left above, she stirs the imagination. This door when completed—the illustration represents only a part of the design—will be more than usually interesting.

All the shades of blue, made brilliant by much polishing, appear in the curious design for a table-top reproduced at the right above. This design, which dimly suggests the zodiac, is palely illuminated by a silver planet. Of blue lacquer again is the screen, still in an unfinished state, shown in the centre above, where dark blue mountains rear themselves against a paler blue heaven, across which streams a milky way of silver stars.

A. S.

(Left) A person of no less taste than Doucet purchased this screen. It is very striking in colour, being of brilliant red lacquer, with nude figures of dark blue, and just a suggestion of silver in the outline which throws them slightly into relief. The draped mysterious figure is done in silver

"LE MAGICIEN DE LA NUIT" PANEL
Year: c. 1912
Materials
Panel lacquered in shades
of red and blue with mother-of-pearl
inlays

LOTUS TABLE
Year: 1913
Materials
Wood lacquered in dark
green, with tassels and
decorated with ivory and
amber rings
Dimensions
82 x 163 x 64 cm

View of Jacques Doucet's Oriental Cabinet with the Lotus Table. Doucet was much taken with Gray's "Le Magicien de la Nuit" Panel and was quick to visit her studio in order to commission various pieces of lacquered furniture for his home, among them the Lotus Table, the Small Red Lacquer Table and the "Bilboquet" Table.

"LE DESTIN" SCREEN
Year: 1913
Materials
Lacquered wood, dark
red base, motifs in tin
Dimensions
119 x 216 cm (opened)

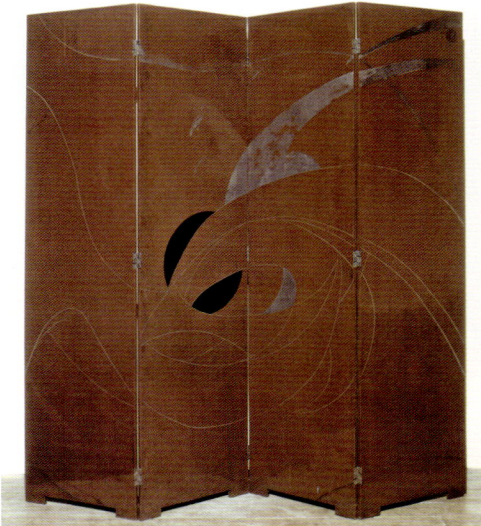

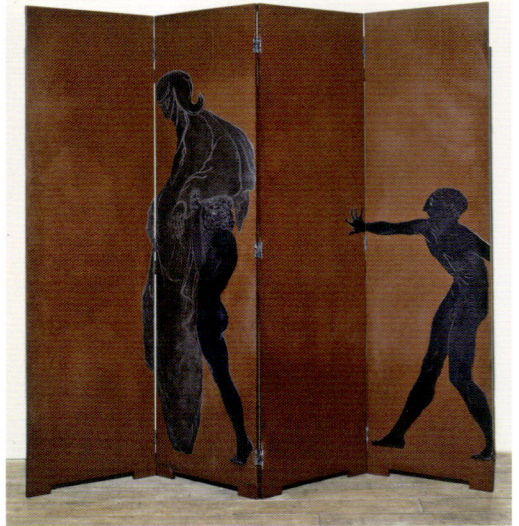

SMALL TABLE
Year: 1915
Materials
Wood lacquered in red
and black
Dimensions
77.5 x 91 x 51 cm

Entrance to Jacques Doucet's home showing the Small Red Lacquer Table.

SIREN CHAIR
Year: c. 1913
Materials
›Structure: black-lacquered wood
›Back: lacquered wood with a carved mermaid and seahorse
›Seat: cushion with fabric upholstery
Dimensions
87.5 x 62 x 51 cm

"BILBOQUET" TABLE
Year: 1915
Materials
›Structure: legs made of wood lacquered in black and silver with sculpted geometrical motifs
›Base and top: wood lacquered in black

The "Bilboquet" Table in the drawing room of Jacques Doucet's home.

Year: c. 1920
Materials
Wood lacquered in black,
red or brown
Dimensions
›Bowl: height 15 cm, diam.
24 cm
›Plates: diam. 16.5 cm
›Pot with lid and base:
height 15 cm, diam. 24 cm
›Box: height 15 cm, diam.
9.75 cm

View of the apartment on Rue Bonaparte in Paris where
Eileen Gray lived until her death.

LACQUER SCREEN IN
SIX SECTIONS WITH
GEOMETRICAL
MOTIFS)
Year: 1922-1925
Materials
Wood lacquered in dark
brown with pale
incisions
Dimensions
199 x 260 cm

LACQUER BLACK AND
SILVER SCREEN IN EIGHT
SECTIONS
Year: 1922-1925
Materials
Lacquered wood with
textured lacquer and silver
leaf decoration

FURNITURE FOR THE LOTA APARTMENT

Year: 1919-1922
Location Rue de Lota,
Paris

Furniture
PIROGUE DAYBED
OSTRICH-EGG LAMP
LACQUER TABLE
BOOKCASE
LOTA SOFA
SERPENT CHAIR
LACQUER SCREENS
DAYBED
HANGING LAMP

The refurbishment of the Lota Apartment was Eileen Gray's first opportunity to undertake a complete décor project. It involved paneling the walls and changing the lighting, decoration and furnishings. Her idea was to cover the walls with lacquer panels, thus hiding the original moldings and creating a dark, intimate and exotic atmosphere through the combination of the new lacquered furnishings and the old and primitive furniture already in place. Her most novel solution was in the main corridor, where she used hundreds of small rectangular lacquered panels, positioning them as if laying bricks. At a certain point along the corridor, the panels opened up perpendicularly to the wall, creating a change in spatial perception and breaking up the extremely long corridor. This was to lead to the idea of the "block" or "brick" screens as independent elements in arranging the distribution of spaces (2).

The abstract geometrical motifs in Gray's rugs can also be seen in the Ostrich-egg Lamp and the lamp made of parchment.

The most surprising design in this apartment, however, was the Pirogue Daybed. This canoe-shaped sofa bed combined the textures of the brown lacquer of the exterior and the silver of the interior and was supported by twelve small arches.

Madame Mathieu-Lévy on the Pirogue Daybed. Photograph taken by Baron Adolf de Meyer for an advertisement for a new perfume.

PIROGUE DAYBED

Year: 1920-1922

Materials

›Exterior: wood lacquered chestnut brown with a scraped treatment creating a tortoiseshell effect
›Interior: wood lacquered silver grey
›Cushions: matt gold upholstery

OSTRICH-EGG LAMP

Year: 1920-1922

Materials

›Cylinder: perforated cork and band of wood lacquered brown
›Lower part: ostrich egg

Dimensions

Length 31.5 cm

LACQUER TABLE
Year: 1920-1922
Materials
>Structure and top:
wood lacquered brown
and silver

BOOKCASE
Year: 1920-1922
Materials
>Structure: wood
lacquered chestnut
brown, grey and silver
>Back: finished in suede
leather
>Adjustable shelves:
lacquered wood

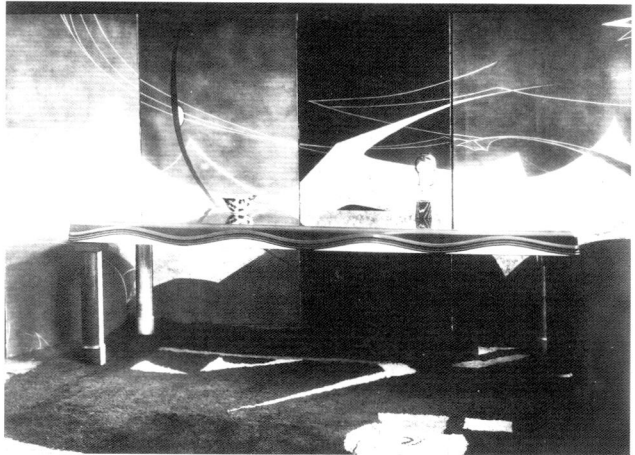

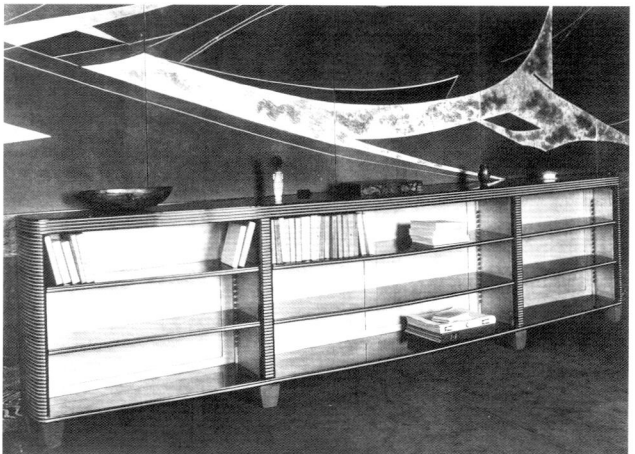

LOTA SOFA
Year: 1923
Materials
›Structure: wood
lacquered black
›Seat and cushions:
fabric upholstery
Dimensions
87 x 240 x 90 cm

Variants
Sofa for Gray's
apartment on Rue
Bonaparte (c. 1930),
which had different
colored upholstery and
feet (1)

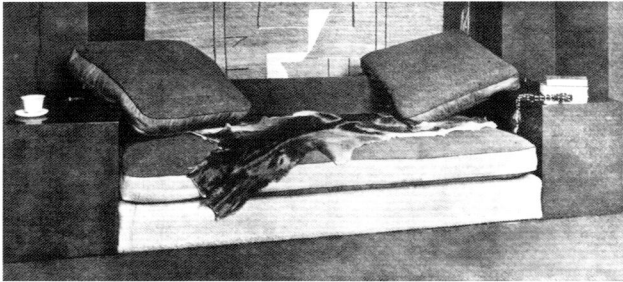

(1)

SERPENT CHAIR
Year: 1920-1922
Materials
›Structure and armrests:
carved wood lacquered
red and yellow
›Seat and back:
upholstered in salmon-
colored fabric or brown or
white leather

LACQUER SCREENS
Year: 1919-1922
Materials
›Rectangular pieces of
lacquered wood
Dimensions
Height 214 cm
Variants
›Screens made of
lacquered blocks (brick
screen), 1925 (2)

Redecoration, done by Paul Ruaud in 1933,
incorporating Eileen Gray's furnishings.

2

DAYBED
Year: 1920-1922
Materials
›Structure: wood
lacquered brown,
orange and silver with
incised decoration
›Seat and cushions:
various types of
upholstery available
Dimensions
70 x 196 x 95.5 cm

HANGING LAMP
Year: 1920
Materials
›Parchment decorated
in red, white and ivory
Dimensions
Length 31.5 cm

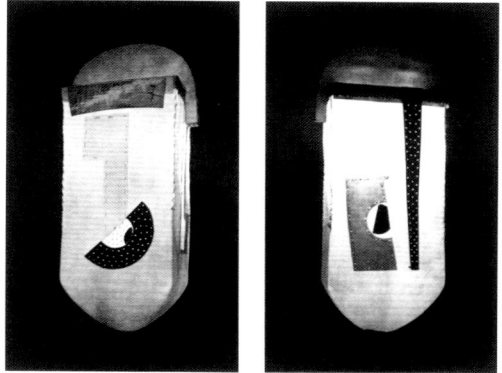

SATELLITE HANGING LAMP

Year: 1919
Materials
Lacquered metal
Dimensions
Diam. 48 cm
Variants
Second version for
Gray's home on Rue
Bonaparte

Eileen Gray designed this lamp for use inside the palace of Prince Yashwantrao Holkar Bahadur, who was crowned in 1925 as the new Maharaja of Indore, a former kingdom near Mumbai, India. It took four years to build the palace, known as "The Garden of Rubies". The most notable spaces in the palace were the prince's own apartment, the banqueting hall, ballroom, music room and the numerous guest rooms. Most of the furniture was designed by Eckart Muthesius, who accompanied the prince on a trip to Paris to find other designers to contribute to the project. The designers they chose included Bruno da Silva, Le Corbusier, Charlotte Perriand and Eileen Gray. The pieces that Gray provided for the palace were two of her Transat Chairs, and the lamp. Three shiny hanging rings 'float' in the space and capture the indirect light cast on them by the three cones positioned between them. Gray later designed another version of this lamp for her home on Rue Bonaparte in Paris.

MONTE CARLO
BEDROOM-BOUDOIR

Year: 1923
Location
Salon des Artistes
Décorateurs, Marzan
Pavilion, Paris

Furniture
SOFA-BED
DESK
CEILING LAMP
JAPANESE-STYLE LAMP
STANDARD LAMP WITH
CUBIST BASE

In 1923, Eileen Gray submitted her interior design for a bedroom to the 14th Salon des Artistes Décorateurs in Paris, presenting a space suitable not only for sleeping in but also as a living area and somewhere to read and write. Taking this idea as her starting point, and also to give her design an air of exoticism, she added the term 'boudoir' to the title of her exhibition. Her furniture designs contain daring, often "disturbing", reminiscences of Cubism and De Stijl. Some of her designs, such as the lamps, were the subject of heated debate, since they were regarded as excessively extravagant and subversive. Nevertheless, even though Gray used rich materials in a diversity of colors, she managed to maintain a deliberate formal restraint, producing an austere and harmonious atmosphere that revealed her enormous talent and sensitivity. She thus began to distance herself from any luxurious hint of French Art Deco and as a result was warmly praised by the Dutch Avant-garde, including architects of the standing of Sybold van Ravesteyn and J.J.P. Oud.

SOFA BED
Year: 1920-1922
Materials
›Structure: black-
lacquered wood,
supported by feet
sculpted in plaster
›Upholstery: leather
cushions

DESK
Year: 1920-1922
Materials
Lacquered wood and
ivory knobs
Dimensions
75 x 161 x 99 cm
Collaborator
Inagaki (design of the
ivory knobs)

CEILING LAMP
Year: 1923
Materials
African-style parchment

JAPANESE-STYLE
LAMP
Year: 1923
Materials
Metal rectangular
structure with
blue-stained and
silvered glass
Variant
Japanese-style lamps,
1925-1930 (1)

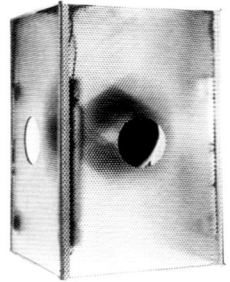

(1)

STANDARD LAMP WITH
CUBIST BASE
Year: 1920-1923
Materials
›Base: painted wood
›Column: metal
›Lamp: paper
Dimensions
Height 1.63 cm
Variants
Lamp with swiveling
stand (1935) (2)

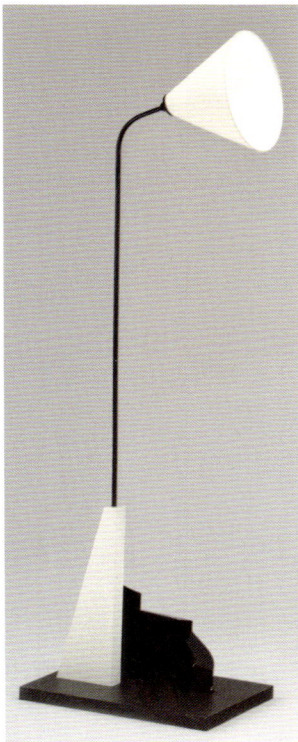

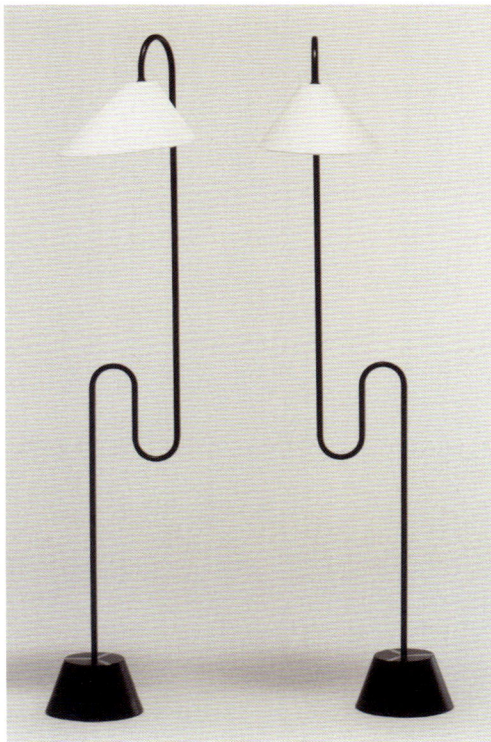

(2)

FURNITURE FOR THE JEAN DÉSERT FURNITURE SHOWROOM

Year: 1922-1930

Location
Rue du Faubourg
Saint-Honoré, Paris

Collaborator
Jean Badovici
(contributed to the
remodeling of the gallery)

Furniture
CIRCULAR RUG
DIVAN
SMALL TABLE
DRESSING TABLE
SOFA BED
ARCHITECT'S CABINET
DE STIJL SIDE TABLE
ARMCHAIR
WOODEN BENCH

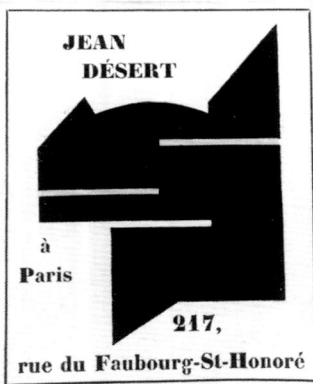

JEAN
DÉSERT

à
Paris

217,
rue du Faubourg-St-Honoré

Invitation to the Galerie Jean Désert, designed by
Chana Orloff.

In May 1922, Eileen Gray opened the Galerie Jean Désert, where she showed and sold her work. With the help of the architect Jean Badovici, she transformed the classical stucco façade into an eye-catching black and white frontage with large openings.

The furniture she hoped to sell in her new gallery was to be very different to her earlier pieces, which she regarded as too individualistic and associated with wealth and frivolity. Influenced, like many of her contemporaries, by Adolf Loos' essay "Ornament and Crime", she began to cast about for cleaner forms, cheaper materials and simpler finishes. And inspired by the ideas of El Lissitzky, Tatlin and Rodchenko, she set about designing objects and light furniture that could be mass-produced, furniture that she believed was capable of changing society's lifestyle. In her designs, she succeeded in ensuring that art was not secondary to functionalism and was able to meld the two concepts.

In the early days, Gray's best-selling items were rugs with abstract designs, but she soon attracted distinguished clients from the world of culture and politics and sold large amounts of furniture of every kind.

Display at the Galerie Jean Désert featuring the
divan, the portable side table, the sofa bed and
small wooden table standing on the circular rug.

(1)

DIVAN
Year: 1925-1928
Materials
›Structure: chrome-
finish tubular steel
›Seat and back:
upholstered in black
leather
Dimensions
60 x 270 x 95 cm

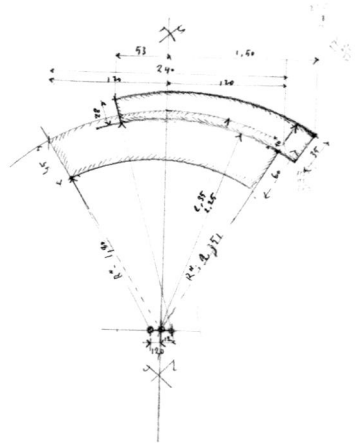

SMALL TABLE
Year: 1925-1928
Materials
›Base: painted wood
›Structure: painted
wood and metal plates
›Top: lacquered wood
Dimensions
32.5 x 52 x 50 cm

DRESSING TABLE
Year: c. 1920
Materials
›Structure: ebanized
oak (fronts) and
sycamore wood
›Pivoting drawers with
ivory knobs
Dimensions
71.5 x 63 x 41 cm

SOFA BED
Year: 1925-1928
Materials
> Structure: chrome-
finish tubular steel
> Seat and back:
upholstered in black
leather
Dimensions
41 x 194 x 87 cm (height
of tubular steel: 61 cm)

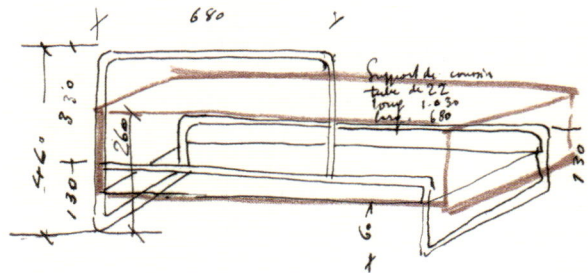

ARCHITECT'S CABINET
Year: c. 1925
Materials
›Structure and
drawers: sycamore
wood
›Knobs: chrome-finish
steel
Dimensions
121 x 205 x 49 cm

Gray designed this cabinet for the architect Henri Pacon.

DE STIJL SIDE TABLE
Year: c. 1923
Materials
Oak and sycamore wood
Dimensions
70 x 56 x 65 cm; height
of lower top: 50 cm

ARMCHAIR
Year: c. 1920
Materials
›Structure: wood
›Seat and back: white
and black leather

WOODEN BENCH
Year: 1920-1922
Materials
›Structure: ebony
plywood with strip of
pale mahogany running
lengthwise
›Central section of the
seat: leather
Dimensions
50 x 96 x 31.5 cm

AEROPLANE HANGING LAMP

Year: 1925-1928
Materials
›Structure: chrome-finish steel with rubber fixings
›Shades: two stacked sheets of opal glass, one of them white, the other blue
›Light source: two neon tubes
Dimensions
Height 19 cm, hanging support 44 cm
›Sheet of white glass: 43 x 37 cm
›Sheet of blue glass: 43 x 33 cm

Eileen Gray developed unprecedented forms for her lamps. The Aeroplane Lamp is an excellent example of her creative ingenuity, and is also a design that refects her interest in aviation. She was one of the first passengers to fly on an airmail plane from Mexico City to Acapulco.

This lighting device consisted of two sheets of opal glass, one white and one blue, arranged one on top of the other and fixed to a metal structure that contained the lighting system consisting of two neon tubes. Five of these lamps were made, some of which were acquired by the Maharaja of Indore and later auctioned by Sotheby's in 1980. One of the versions of this design is to be found in the master bedroom of Eileen Gray's apartment on Rue Bonaparte in Paris.

FURNISHINGS FOR E.1027

Year: 1926-1929
Location
Cap Martin,
Roquebrune, Côte
d'Azur (France)
Collaborator
Jean Badovici

Furniture

FURNISHINGS FOR
LA SALLE:
CURVED CUPBOARD
TRANSAT CHAIR
"BIBENDUM" CHAIR
CABINET WITH
PIVOTING DRAWERS
NON-CONFORMIST
CHAIR
DINING TABLE
BLUE MARINE RUG
CENTIMETRE RUG

FURNISHINGS FOR
THE STUDIO-
BEDROOM:
DRESSING CABINET
BATHROOM MIRROR
WALL LIGHTS

FURNISHINGS FOR
THE GUEST ROOM:
E.1027 TABLE
WARDROBE
SATELLITE MIRROR

MOVABLE FURNITURE:
FOLDING TEA TABLE
TROLLEY TABLE

Eileen Gray described her first completed project for a house as being "for a person who likes *work*, *sports* and receiving friends."

In her design, she ensured the various spaces remained separate—an approach that she regarded as a priority—by grouping the various areas of the home around the staircase and circulation area, keeping them independent of each other while at the same time giving them an outdoor area of their own. The house is small, with a surface area of just 150 m², yet all the rooms and other areas feel spacious.

In keeping with the Mediterranean setting, she used maritime motifs, as found in the handrails, built-in headboards for the bed, blue canvas for awnings and hammocks, and so on.

In her designs, she explored every possible use that a piece of furniture could be put to and sought to achieve maximum flexibility. As a consequence, a single gesture was all it took to transform one of her pieces. Even though she retained her sense of practicality, she arrived at remarkable aesthetically attractive solutions, for example, through the bending and folding of elements, which was a hallmark of her designs. Her liking for factory production techniques is also revealed in the use of prefabricated components in her screens and windows, and even the doors.

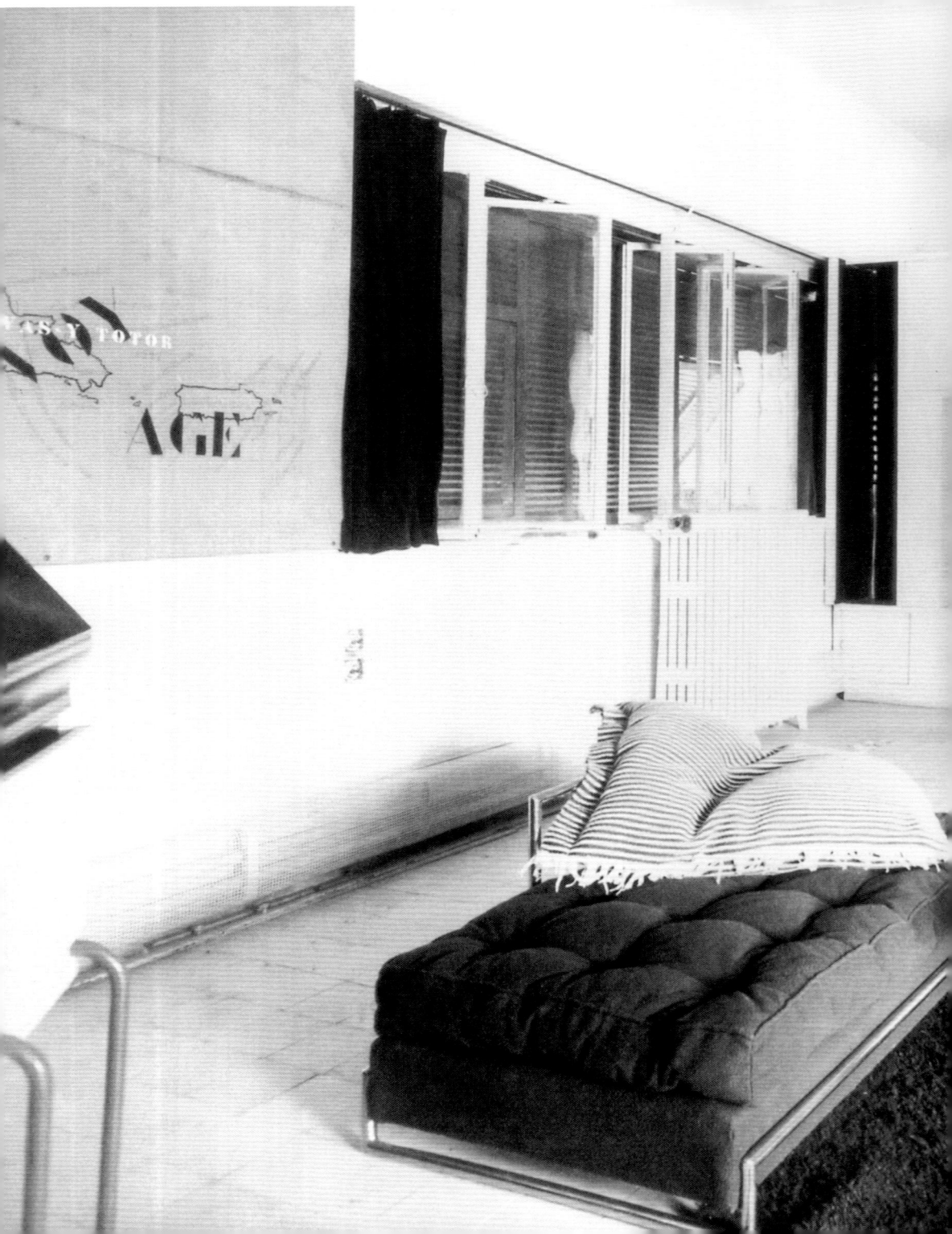

TRANSAT CHAIR
Year: 1925-1930
Materials
›Structure: plywood
with nickel-plated fixings
and finishing details
›Seat and back:
upholstered in black
leather
Dimensions
76 x 54 x 98 cm

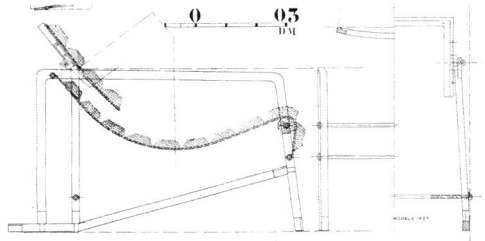

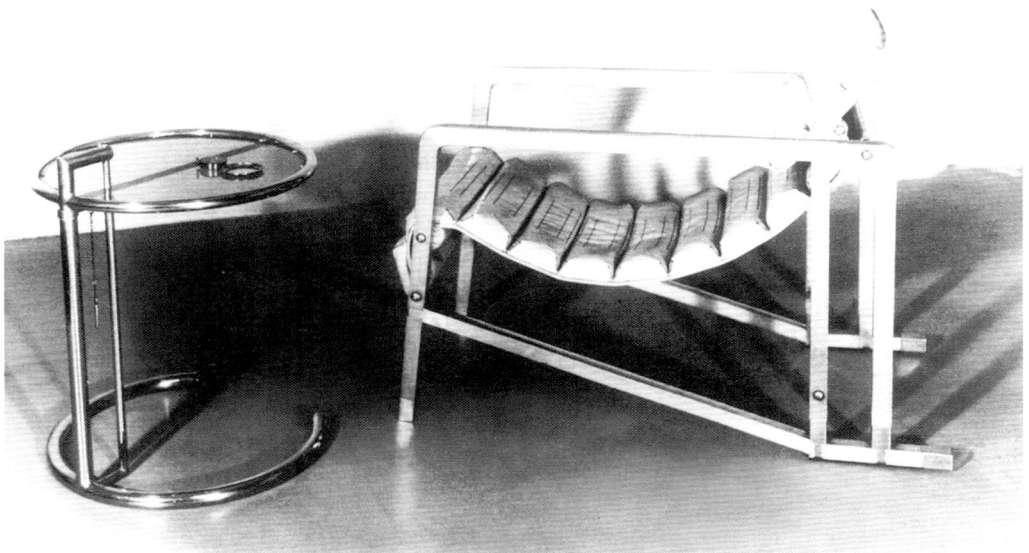

"BIBENDUM" CHAIR
Year: 1925-1926
Materials
›Structure: chrome-
finish tubular steel
›Seat and back:
upholstered in white
leather
Dimensions
73 x 90 x 83 cm

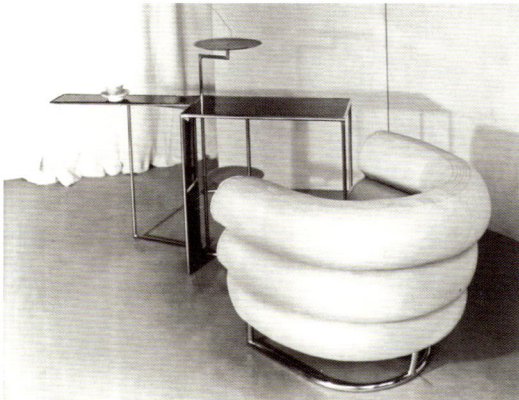

CABINET WITH
PIVOTING DRAWERS
Year: 1926-1929
Materials
>Structure and
drawers: painted wood
Dimensions
63 x 73.2 x 27 cm

NON-CONFORMIST
CHAIR
Year: 1926-1929
Materials
›Structure: chrome-
finish tubular steel
›Seat and back:
fabric upholstery
Dimensions
77 x 62 x 57 cm

Earlier versions
›Asymmetrical Chair,
prototype (1926-29) (1)
›Chair with symmetrical
armrests (1926-29) (2)

One of the armrests of the Non-conformist
Chair was eliminated to give greater freedom by
offering the person sitting in the chair two
possible sitting positions.

Sketches of various chairs, among
them the Non-conformist Chair.

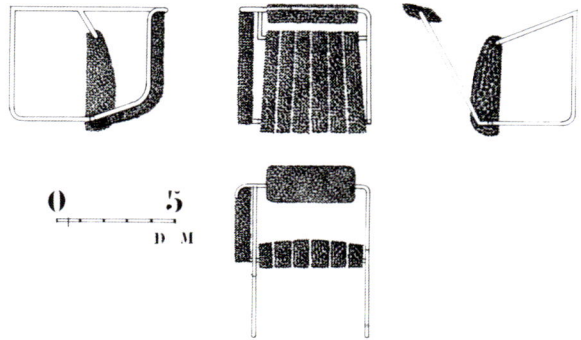

(1)

(2)

DINING TABLE
Year: 1926-1929
Materials
>Structure: tubular steel
>Top: two sections of cork
Dimensions
73 x 115.5 x 63 cm

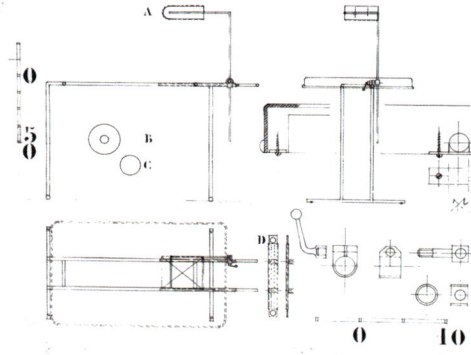

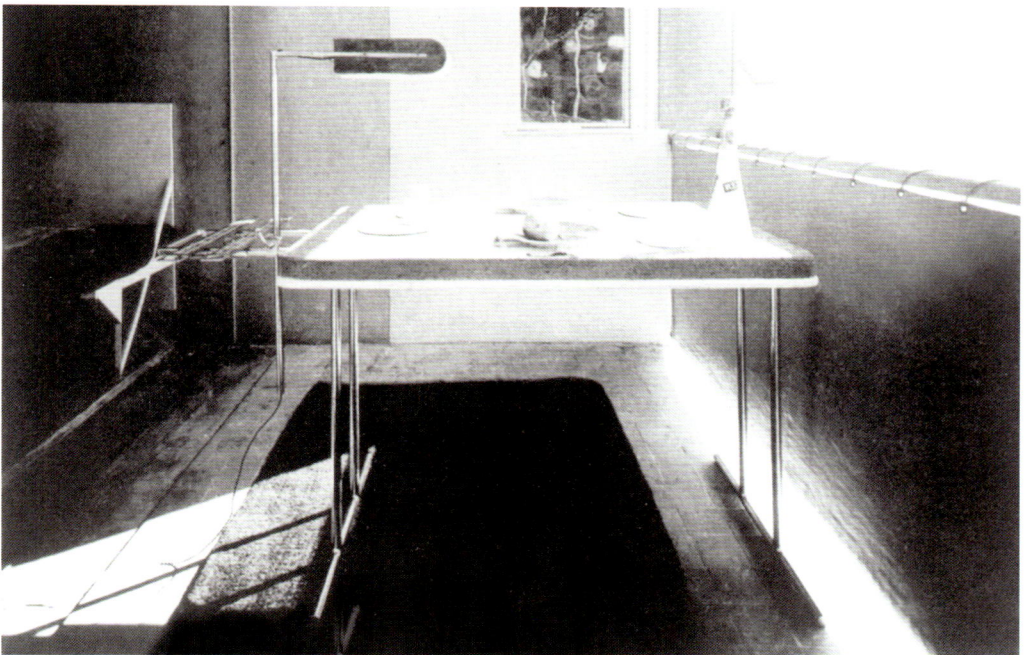

BLUE MARINE RUG
Year: 1926-1929
Materials
Pure wool, hand-woven
Dimensions
215 x 110 cm

CENTIMETER RUG
Year: 1926-1929
The original drawing is
gouache on paper,
16.7 x 14.5 cm

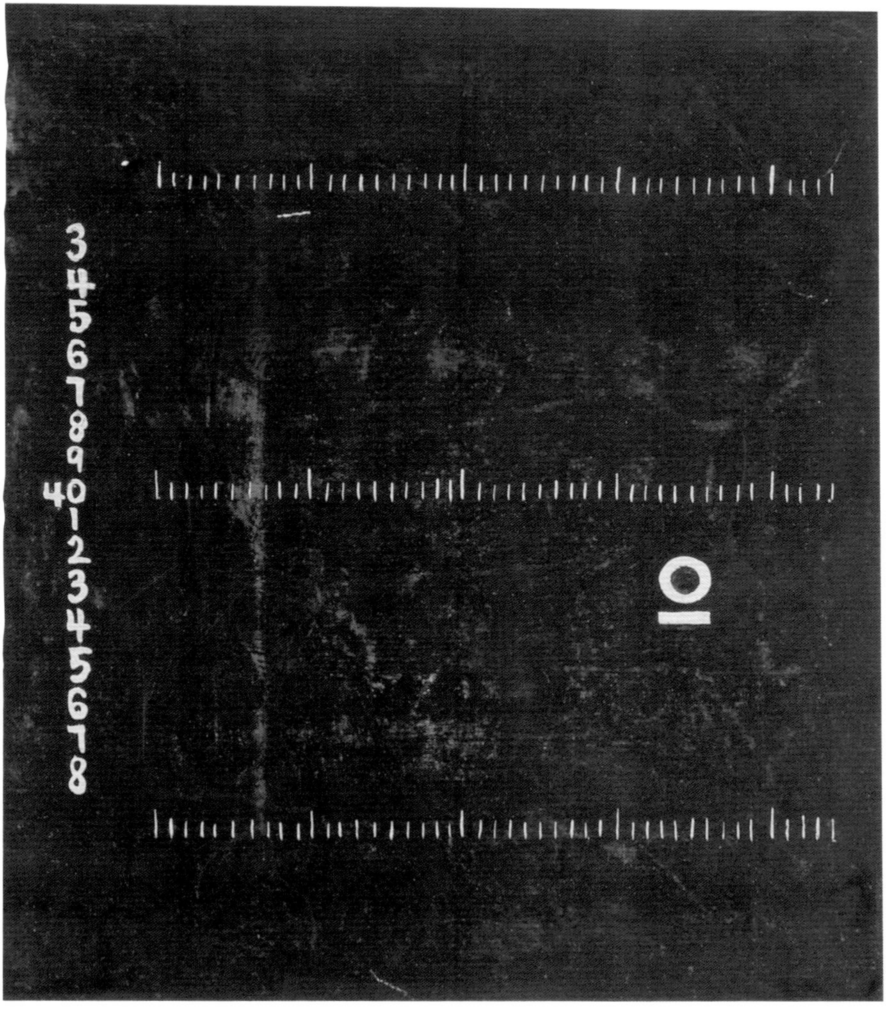

Floor plant of the studio-bedroom.
View of the studio-bedroom with adjustable
writing table.

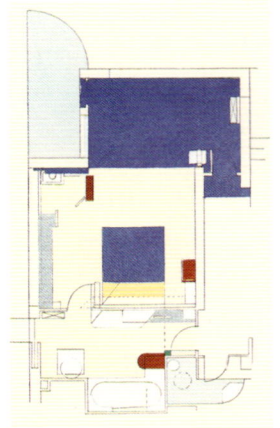

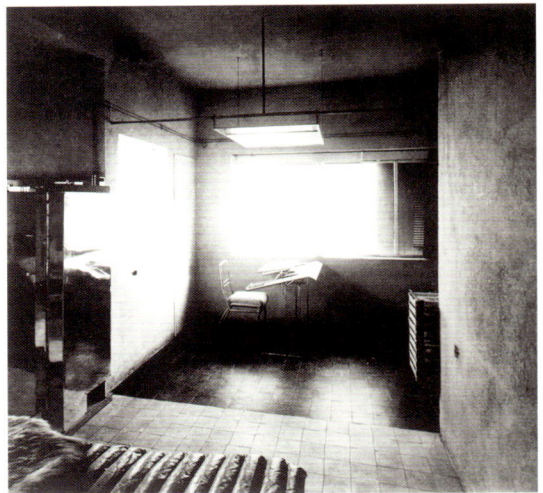

DRESSING CABINET
Year: 1926-1929
Materials
Pine plywood, cork,
aluminum and glass
Dimensions
163 x 55 x 17 cm

BATHROOM MIRROR
Year: 1926-1929
Materials
›Frame: chrome-finish
steel with a swiveling
section
›Mirror: bevel-edged,
silvered glass
Dimensions
63 x 56 cm

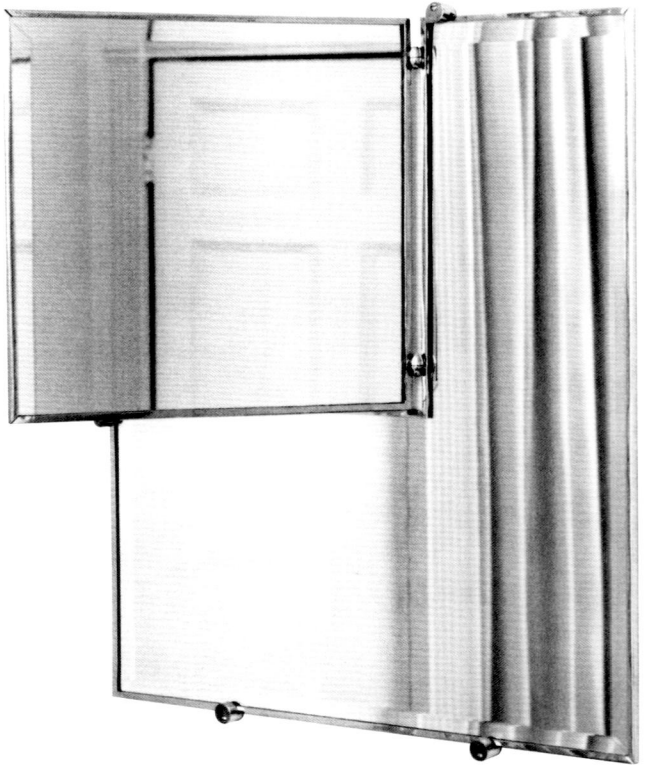

WALL LIGHTS
Year: 1926-1928
Materials
Double cylinder:
chrome-finish steel
Dimensions
8.4 x 12 cm

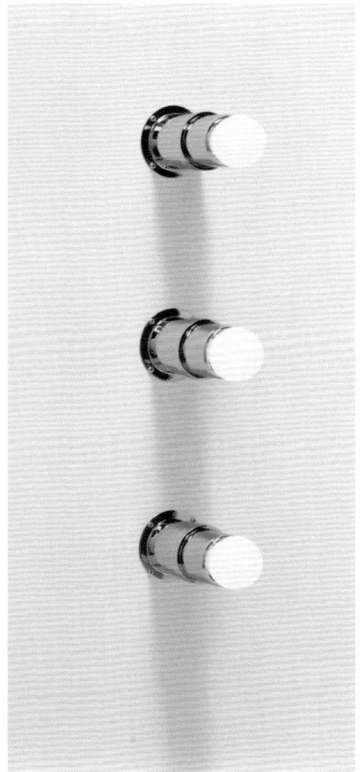

Floor plan of the guest room.

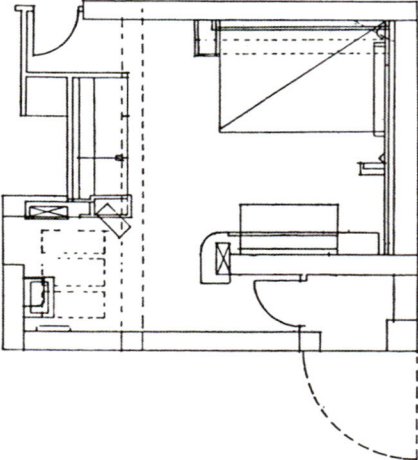

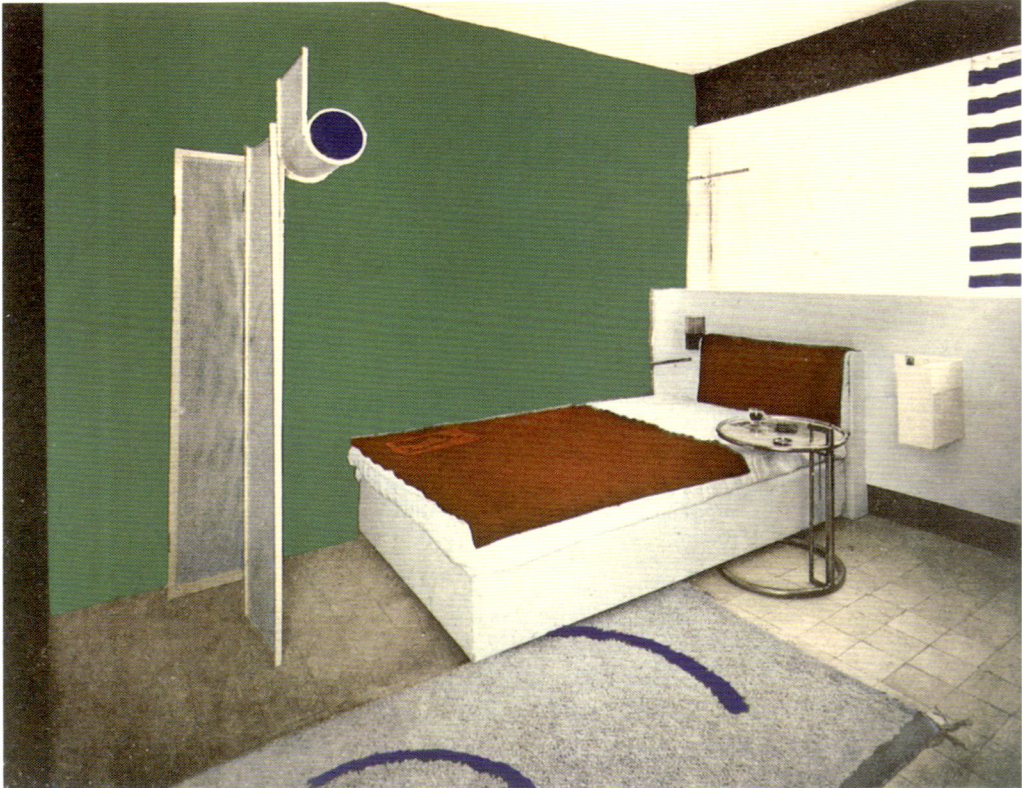

E.1027 TABLE
Year: 1926-1929
Materials
>Structure: chrome-
finish tubular steel,
height-adjustable
>Top: glass
Dimensions
61-62 x 50-51 cm
Variants
Portable tables
(1925-30) (8)

(3)

WARDROBE
Year: 1926-1929
Materials
>Exterior: painted wood
with Ripolin
>Interior: lined with
celluloid, glass shelves,
ceiling made of glass
panels with interior
lighting

DRESSING TABLE
Year: 1925-1930
Materials
›Structure: chrome-
finish tubular steel
›Pivoting drawers:
rosewood
›Top: leather (rosewood
in the second version)
Dimensions
84 x 64 x 47 cm

SATELLITE MIRROR
Year: 1926-1928

FOLDING TEA TABLE
Year: 1926-1929
Materials
›Structure: chrome-finish tubular steel
›Folding and flipping tops: aluminum
Dimensions
101 (total height) x 73-139 x 63.5 cm

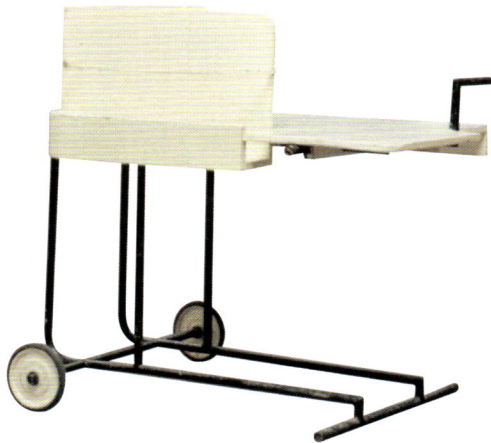

TROLLEY TABLE
Year: 1926-1929
Materials
>Structure: tubular steel
>Top: painted wood
Dimensions
77 x 84 x 52.2 cm

TROLLEY TABLE
Year: 1920
Materials
>Structure: tubular steel
>Top: wood and glass

DOUBLE X TABLE

Year: 1927-1929
Materials
›Structure: tubular
stainless steel
›Top: lacquered plywood
or glass
Dimensions
73 x 224 x 82 cm with
wooden top
71 x 224 x 110 cm with
glass top

Eileen Gray once again made use of the tubular steel structure, a mark of modernity, for a "classic" dining table design. The support for the extremely long top, measuring over two meters in length, proved to be a constructional challenge, since it had to be stable to make it safe when used. The outcome is an elegant and "sincere" crossed structure that reveals the logic of its behavior. It optimizes the overall rigidity of the piece and gives the table its name. The degree of abstraction in the design allowed flexible usage of the table, a feature Gray strove for. It served as both a dining table for a number of people and as an individual desk. The glass top gave this version an appearance of lightness, conveying a curious impression of weightlessness.

STUDIO APARTMENT FOR JEAN BADOVICI

Year: 1929-1931
Location
No. 17 on Rue
Chateaubriand, Paris

Furnishings
DESK WITH
ADJUSTABLE LAMP
DIVAN WITH PIVOTING
TABLE
PERFORATED SCREEN
OVERHEAD
CUPBOARDS (2)
SHOWER CURTAIN (3)

Jean Badovici was of Rumanian origin and trained as an architect in Paris. Most of his work revolved around critical commentary, in particular through the publication of the magazine *L'Architecture Vivante*. In Eileen Gray he discovered a woman of enormous talent and they became close friends. In 1930 Gray designed the interiors of his apartment on Rue Chateaubriand in Paris. The entire strategy of the project was a response to the need to make the most of the limited amount of space in the apartment, which measured approximately 40 m² and was further complicated by its trapezoidal floor plan. The conversion was intended to produce a habitable space where the occupant could both work and enjoy his or her leisure time. Thanks to the concentration and reduction of the service areas to the minimum possible, the strategic positioning of mirrors and the dual function of the furnishings, the studio conveyed a tremendous sense of space. This project provided Gray with an ideal opportunity to experiment with movable devices, such as folding stairs, sliding metal curtains, screens and swiveling mirrors. The living room area was a single square space, taking up virtually two thirds of the entire apartment, and measuring almost 3.2 meters up to the ceiling. By the simple device of positioning a bed diagonally across it in the middle, Gray divided the workspace from the rest area.

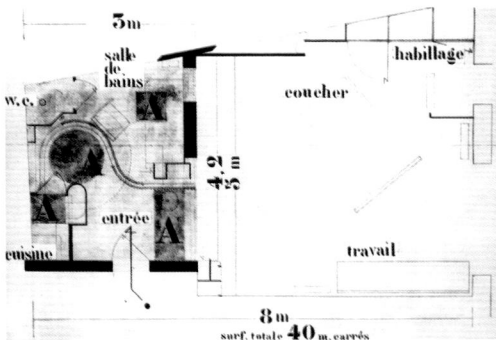

5m
salle de bains
habillage
w.c.
coucher
4.5 m
entrée
travail
cuisine
8m
surf. totale **40** m. carrés

Work area at one end of the room, with the
built-in desk and adjustable light fixed to a cork
notice board.

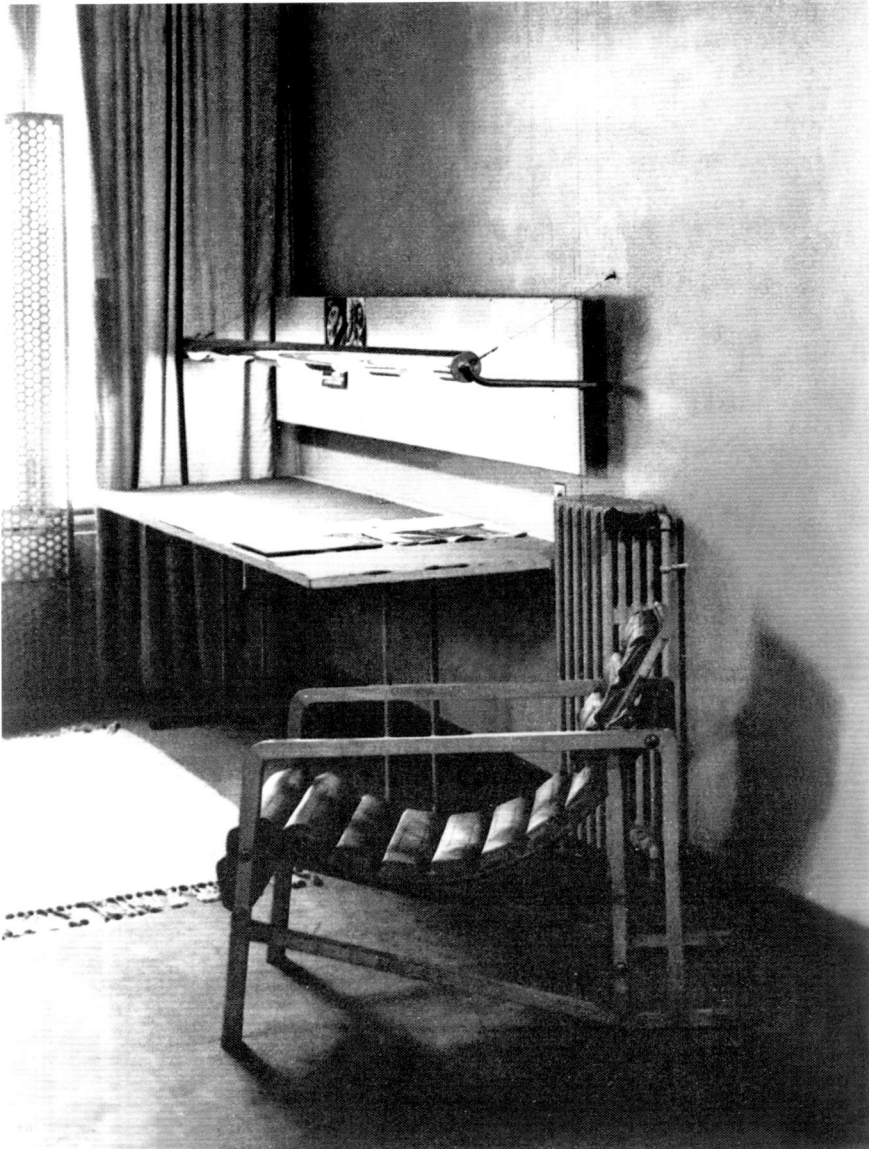

Built into the head of the sofa bed were a clock,
a pencil holder and switches. To the side, it had a
pivoting table for resting books on while reading.

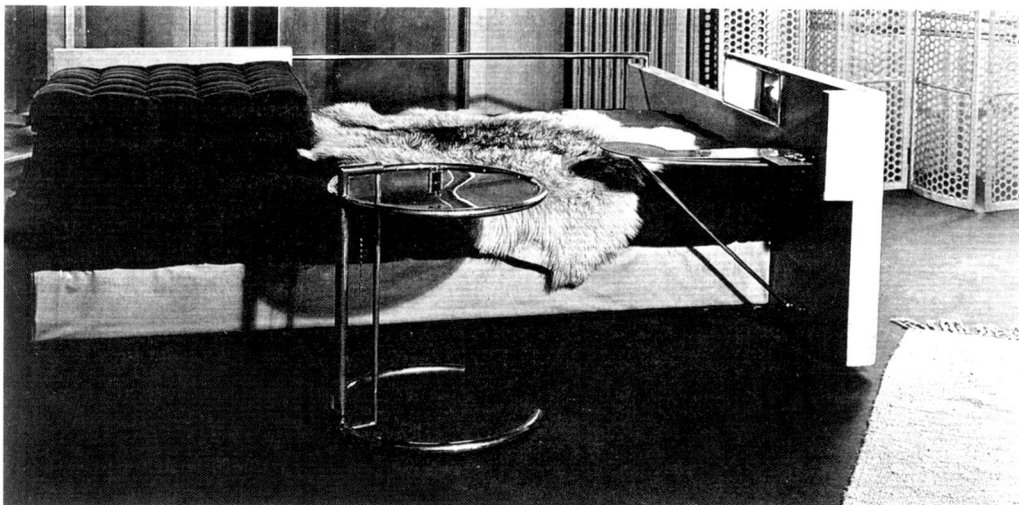

PERFORATED SCREEN
Year: 1926-1929
Materials
Four panels made of painted
wood and sheet metal
Dimensions
1.67 x 1.39 m (opened)
Variant
Celluloid Screen (1931) (1)

(1)

Storage space above the false ceiling.
Metal curtains to conceal the bathroom.

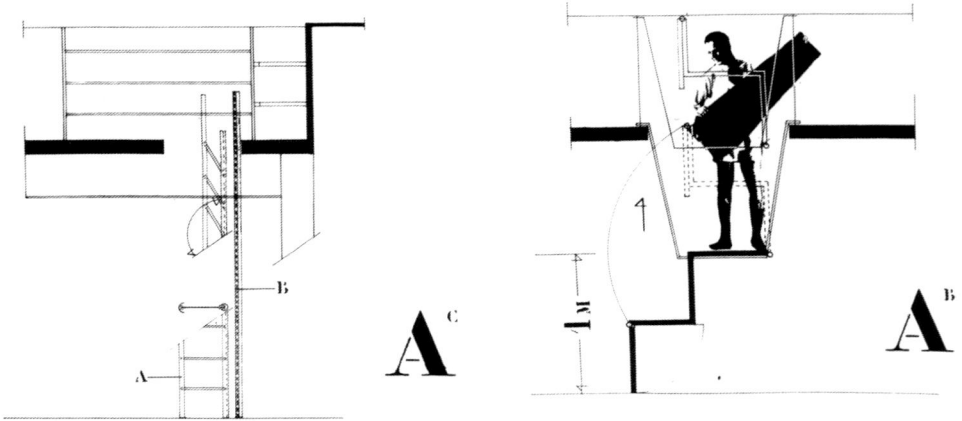

(2)

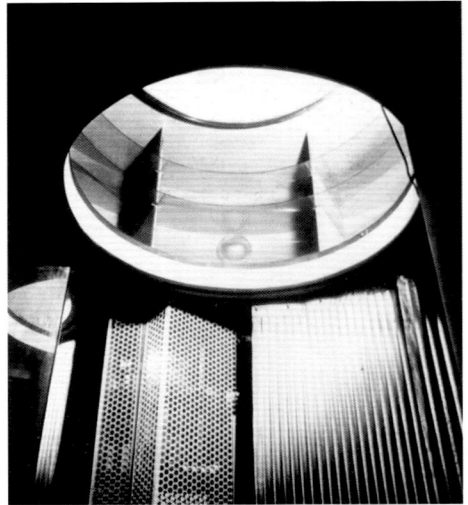

(3)

TUBULAR FLOOR LAMP

Year: 1930
Materials
›Structure: base and
tube made of chrome-
finish steel with plastic
fixings
›Light: pearl tungsten
tube
Dimensions
103 x 25 cm (diam.)

The forceful essentiality of this lamp design has made it timeless. In this case, Gray expressly selected the optimum materials to create a simple standard lamp. Following on from what she called "the sins of my past," she began to move towards factory furniture production. As a result, she used tubular steel in a number of her furnishing designs, in keeping with the trends set by the Modern Movement. Even so, she refused to abandon her particular way of understanding design.

She always paid careful attention to the manipulation of light, both natural and artificial. With this extremely versatile lamp, easily adaptable to any type of usage or space, she demonstrated her ability to create warm atmospheres by means of low-level lighting.

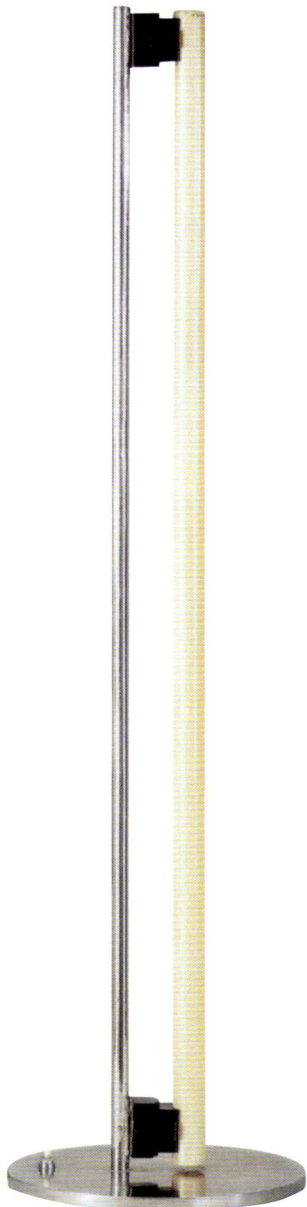

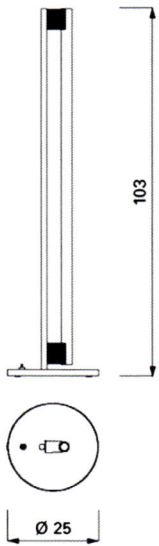

103

Ø 25

FURNISHINGS FOR TEMPE À PAILLA

Year: 1932-1934
Location
Castellar, Provence
(France)

Furniture
CHAIR
OUTDOOR TABLE WITH
TWO POSITIONS
"SIÈGE COIFFEUSE"
CHAIR
CUBIC DRAWER UNIT
WITH PIVOTING
DRAWERS
EXTENDING WARDROBE
DINING TABLE
HEIGHT-ADJUSTABLE
TABLE
THREE VARIANTS OF
TABLE WITH WIRE
FRAME
LOW OUTDOOR
ARMCHAIR
OUTDOOR RECLINER
"S-BEND" CHAIR
BAR STOOLS

Eileen Gray decided to purchase this steeply sloping site with its sweeping views of the Alps for her new home. With white concrete walls constructed on top of the old stone walls of a pre-existing building, the house contrasted with its surroundings while at the same time acquiring a unique visual force.

The interaction that Eileen Gray managed to generate between the interior and exterior areas gave the small house a sense of spaciousness and added to its functional possibilities. This versatility turned the project into the perfect dwelling machine, suited at all times to her needs.

The use of built-in furniture created a tremendous impression of openness in the space. In addition, the furnishings were designed to achieve maximum functionality: they divided spaces, served several functions or could simply be folded up for easy storage and to save space.

In her designs for her house Tempe à Pailla, Gray arrived at a definitive conception of furniture as economical, functional and versatile by stripping it of any refinement.

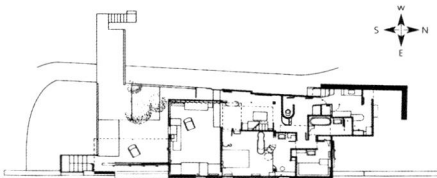

Exterior view of Tempe à Pailla. The name of the house comes from a French proverb concerning the time things need to take to mature and alluded to the Gray's professional evolution in the design of this house.

CHAIR
Year: 1930
Materials
> Structure: chrome-finish tubular steel
> Seat and back: leather or canvas with blue stitching
Dimensions
73.5 x 45 x 55 cm; seat height 47 cm

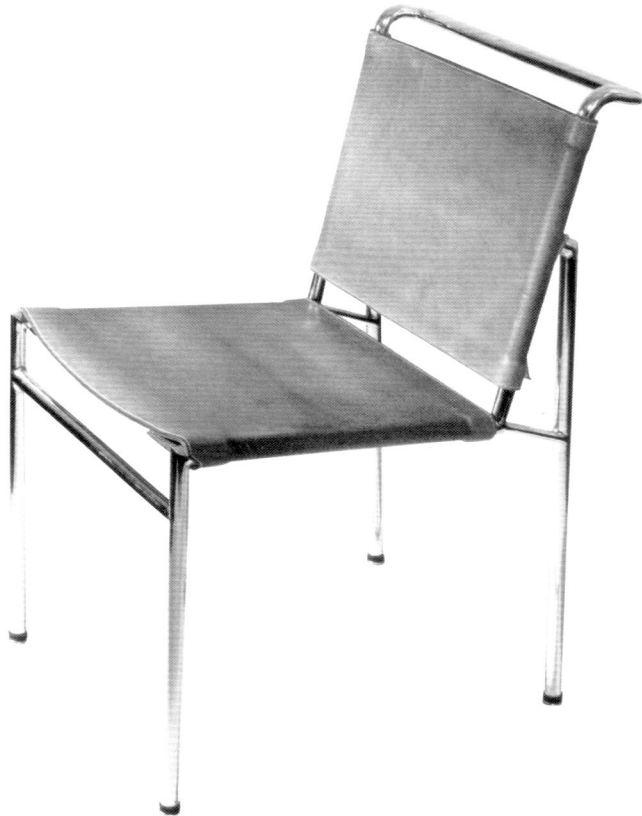

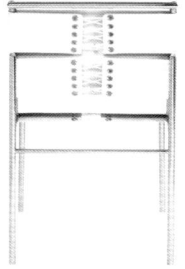

OUTDOOR TABLE WITH
TWO POSITIONS
Year: 1932-1934
Materials
›Structure: metal
›Two-sided top: one side
zinc, the other cork
Dimensions
›Position 1:
42/31.5 x 126 x 65 cm
›Position 2:
65 x 126 x 56 cm

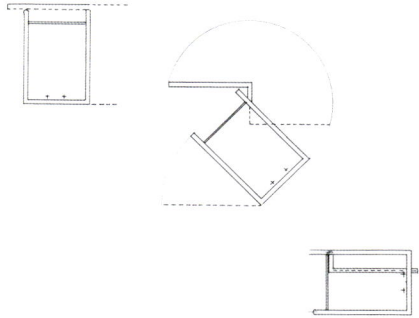

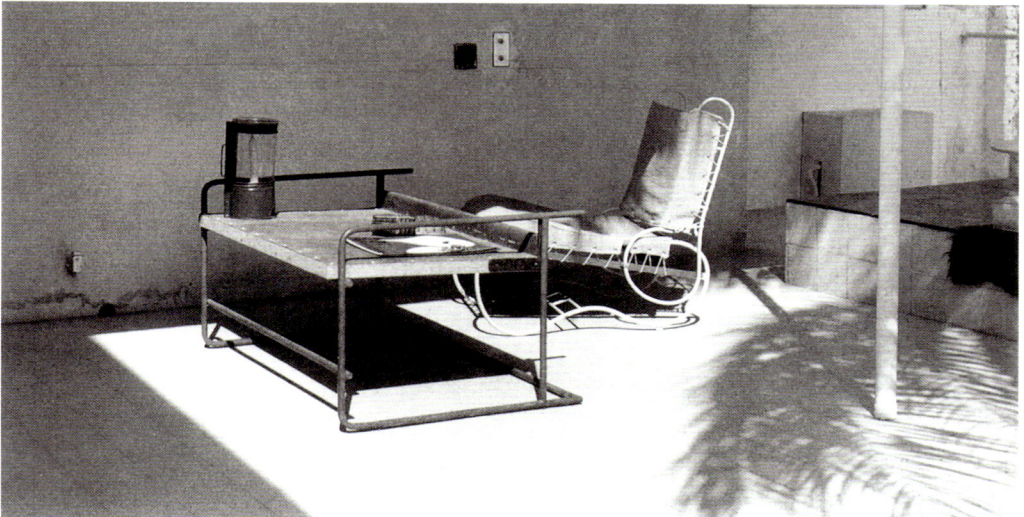

"SIÈGE COIFFEUSE"
CHAIR
Year: 1932-1934
Materials
>Structure: metal

This chair can be converted into a set of steps.

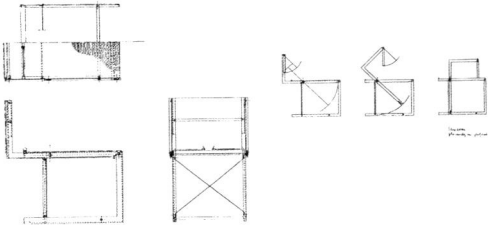

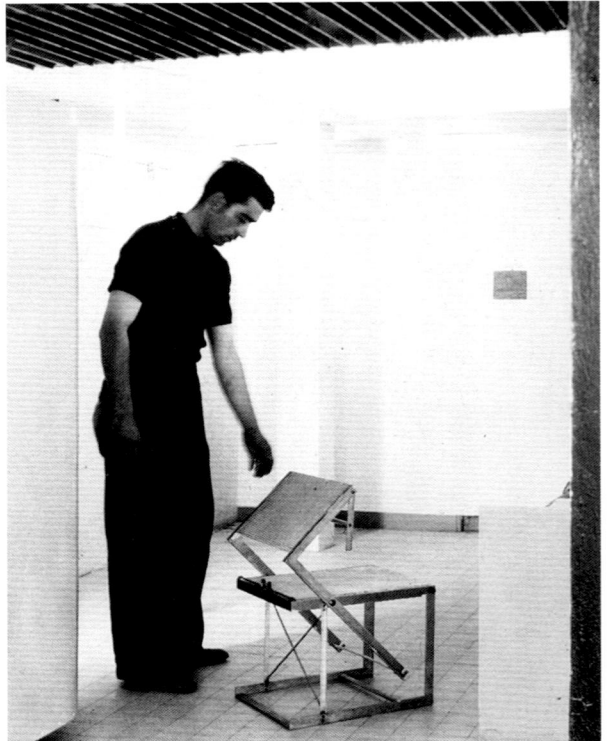

CUBIC DRAWER UNIT WITH
PIVOTING DRAWERS
Year: 1932-1934
Materials
›Structure: metal and wood
›Drawers: wood painted
yellow outside and gray
inside
›Shelves: glass
Dimensions
65 x 52.5 x 46.5 cm

EXTENDING WARDROBE
Year: 1932-1934
Materials
›Structure: extending
metal carcass
›Outer skin: perforated
Plexiglas
›Knob: chrome-finish metal

Master bedroom showing various elements: the
mosquito net over the bed, the extending wardrobe,
the bed head with its sliding light and built-in
switches, and the "Siège coiffeuse" Chair to the left.

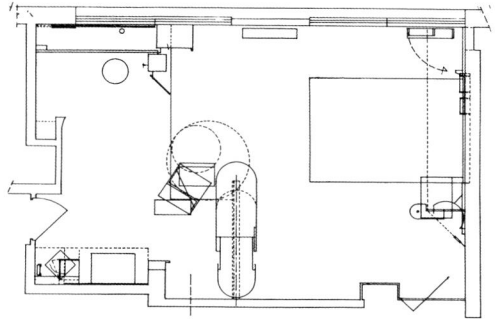

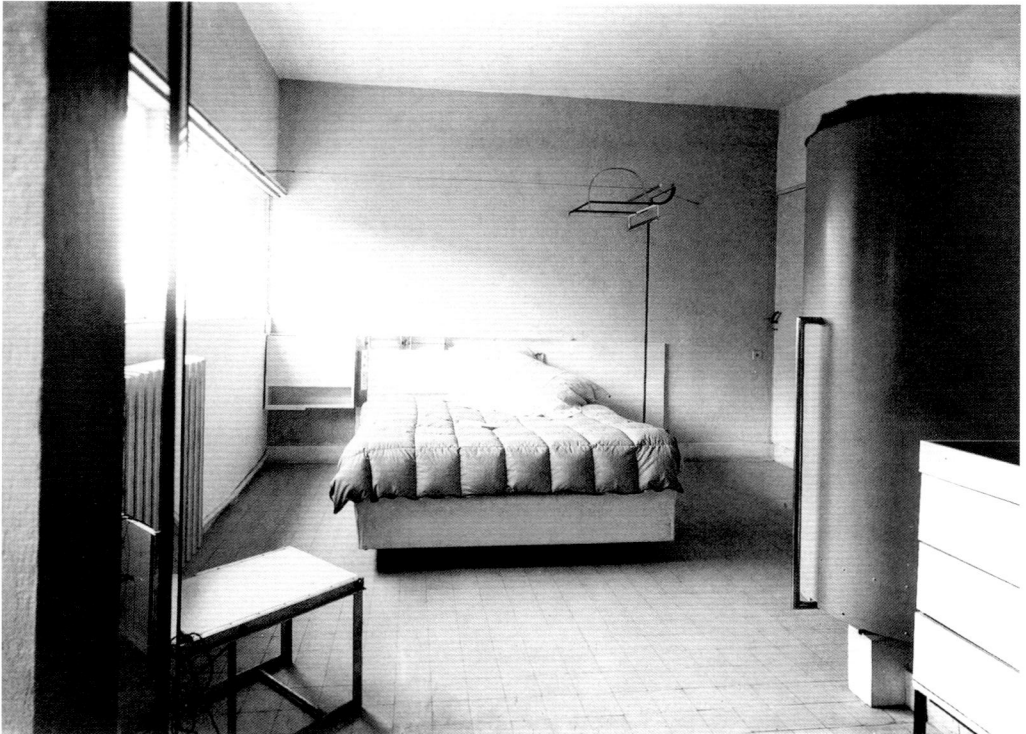

DINING TABLE
Year: 1932-1934
Materials
›Structure: perforated
metal legs
›Top: wood

HEIGHT-ADJUSTABLE
TABLE
Year: 1932-1934
Materials
›Structure: perforated
metal legs with wheels
›Top: wood

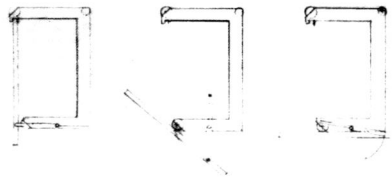

THREE VARIANTS OF
TABLE WITH WIRE
FRAME
Year: 1935
Materials
>Structure: thin tubes
of chrome-finish steel
>Top: wood, some with
low reliefs carved into
the top or finished with
sheet of red copper (1)
Dimensions
44.5 x 98 x 51 cm
40 x 78.5 cm

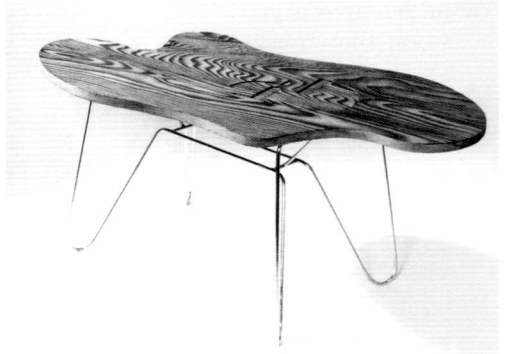

1)

View of the terrace of the Lou Perou
house near Saint-Tropez.

LOW OUTDOOR
ARMCHAIR
Year: 1930
Materials
›Structure: chrome-
finish tubular steel
›Fabric: canvas
Dimensions
Height 71 cm

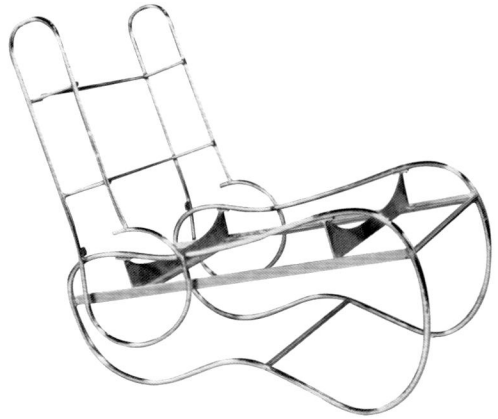

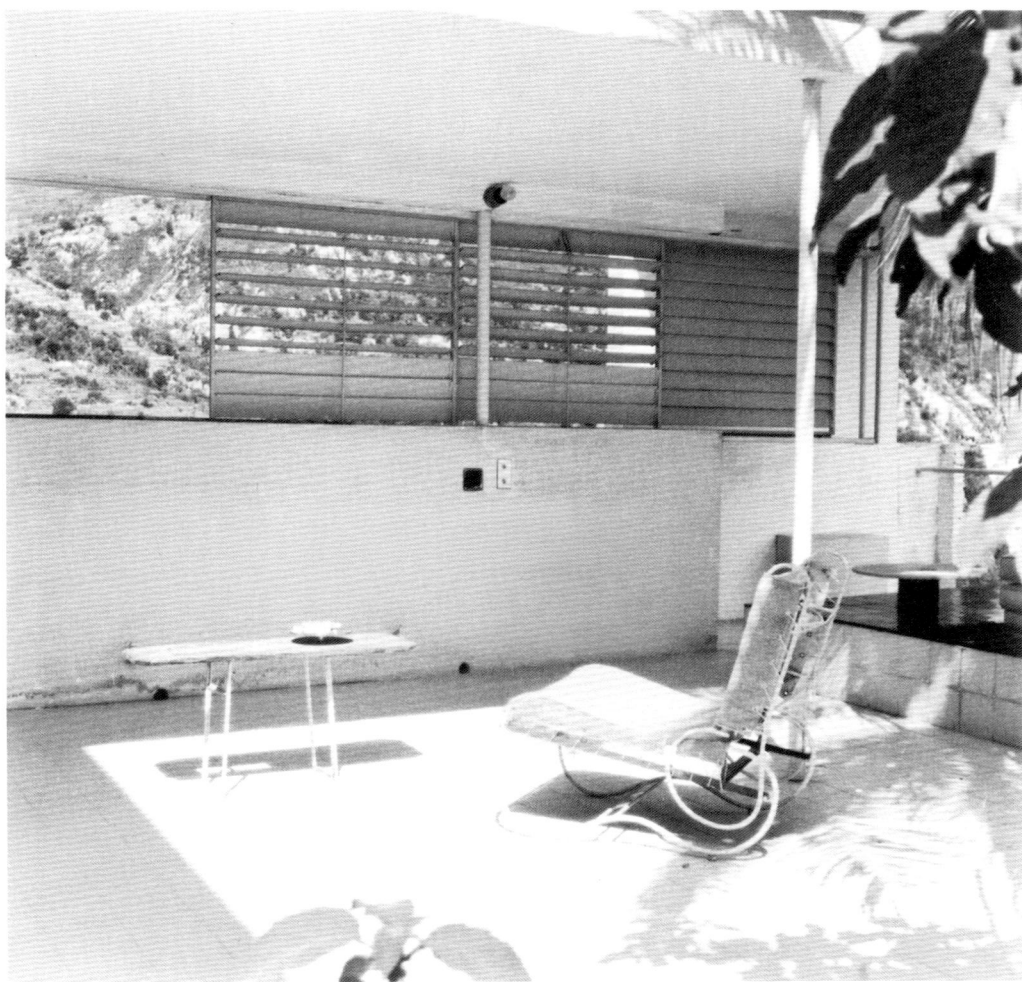

OUTDOOR RECLINER
Year: 1935
Materials
>Structure: black-
painted metal and
plywood
>Seat and back:
fabric cushions

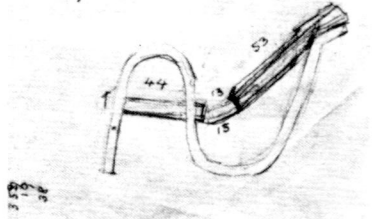

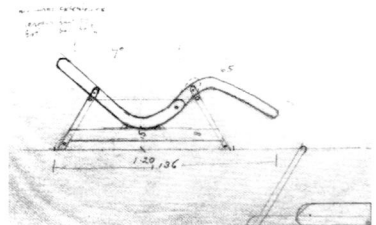

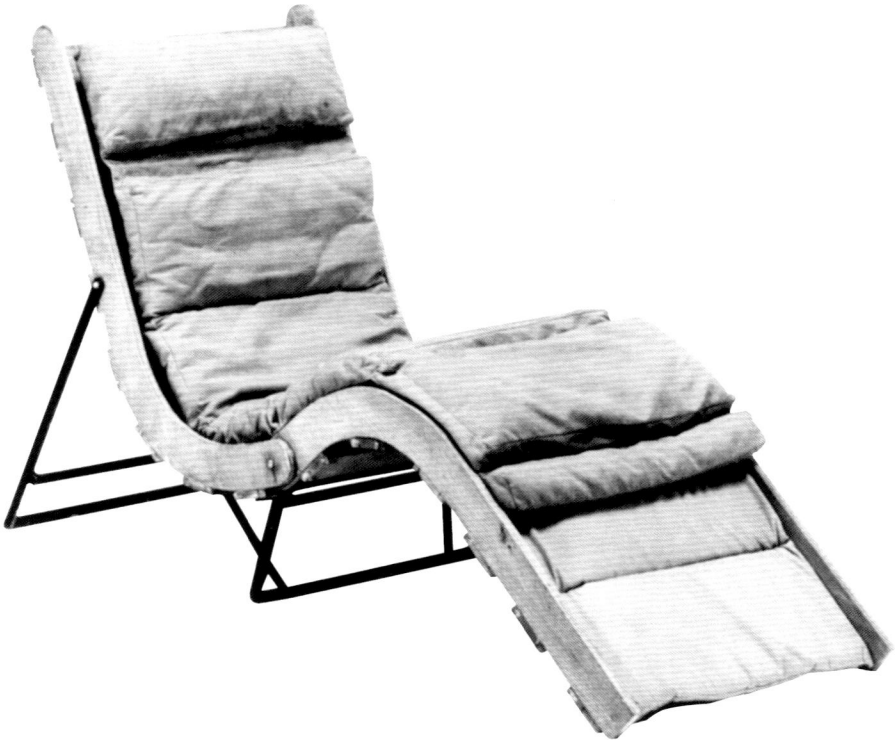

"S-BEND" CHAIR
Year: 1932-1934
Materials
>Structure: wood and
metal mechanisms
>Seat and back: canvas
upholstery
Dimensions
80 x 99 cm

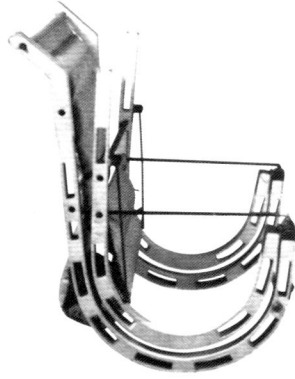

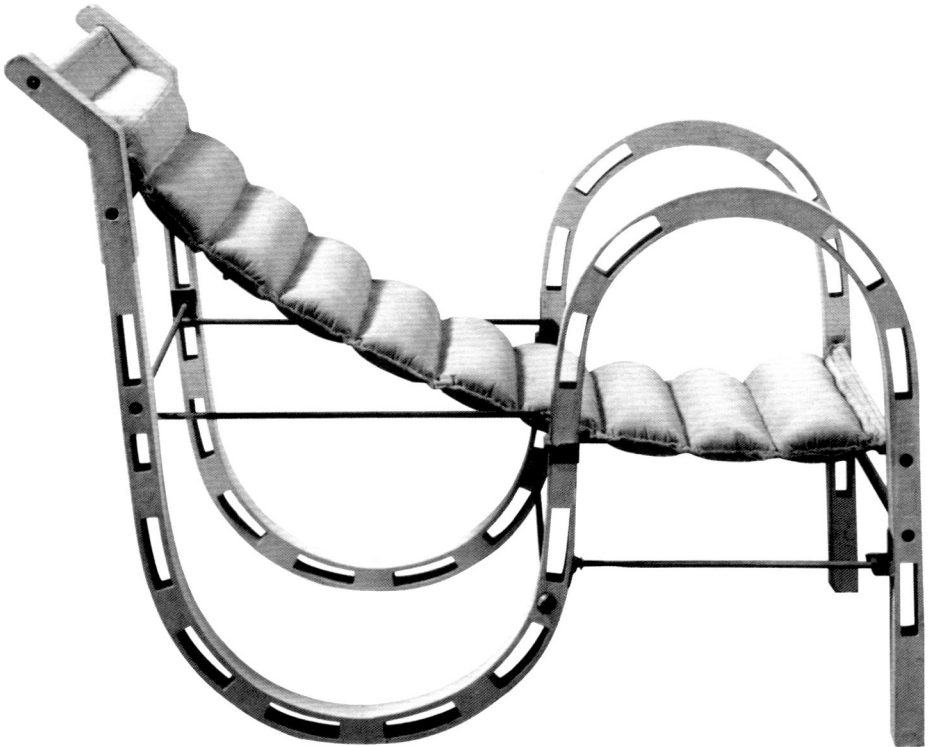

BAR STOOLS
Year: 1926-1929
Materials
›Structure: painted steel
›Seat: black upholstery
Dimensions
73 x 30 x 39.5 cm

CHRONOLOGY

"LE MAGICIEN DE LA NUIT" PANEL
c. 1912
p. 21

LOTUS TABLE
1913
p. 21

SIREN CHAIR
1913
p. 24

"BILBOQUET" TABLE
1915
p. 24

"LE DESTIN" SCREEN
1914
p. 22

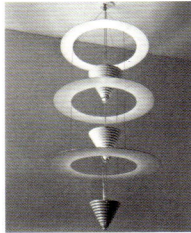

SATELLITE HANGING
LAMP 1919
p. 39

SMALL RED
LACQUER TABLE
1915   p. 23

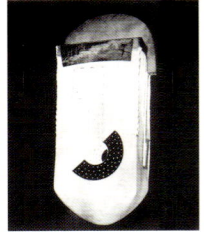

HANGING LAMP
1920
p. 37

LACQUER BOWL
1920
p. 26

LACQUER PLATES
1920
p. 26

LACQUER POT
1920
p. 26

LACQUER BOX
1920
p. 26

ARMCHAIR
1920
p. 51

CIRCULAR RUG
1920
p. 45

TROLLEY TABLE
1920
p. 79

DRESSING TABLE
c. 1920
p. 48

WOODEN BENCH
1920-1922
p. 51

BOOKCASE
1920-1922
p. 31

OSTRICH-EGG
LAMP
1920-1922   p. 30

DAYBED
1920-1922
p. 36

SERPENT CHAIR
1920-1922
p. 33

LACQUER TABLE
1920-1922
p. 31

PIROGUE DAYBED
1920-1922
p. 30

STANDARD LAMP
WITH CUBIST BASE
1920-1923   p. 43

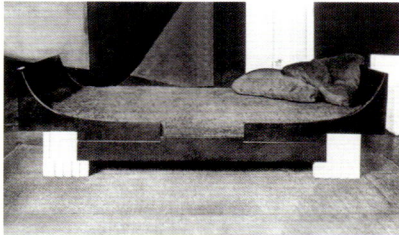

SOFA BED
1920-1922
p. 41

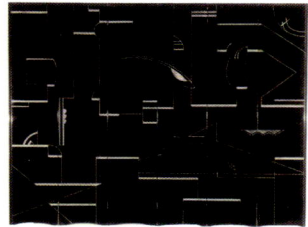

LACQUER SCREEN IN SIX SECTIONS
WITH GEOMETRICAL MOTIFS
1922-1925   p. 27

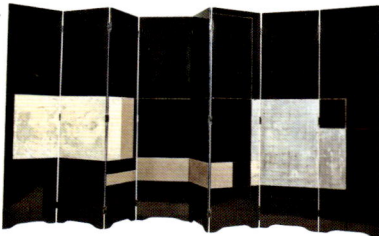

LACQUER BLACK AND SILVER SCREEN IN
EIGHT SECTIONS
1922-1925   p. 27

DESK
1923
p. 41

CEILING LAMP
1923
p. 42

DE STIJL SIDE
TABLE c. 1923
p. 51

LOTA SOFA
1923
p. 32

ARCHITECT'S
CABINET
c. 1925   p. 50

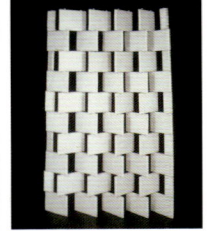

WHITE LACQUER
SCREEN
1925   p. 35

BLACK LACQUER
SCREEN
1925   p. 35

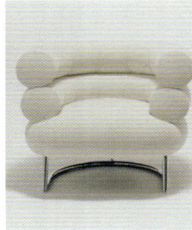

BIBENDUM CHAIR
1925-1926
p. 60

SMALL TABLE
1922-1930
p. 47

DIVAN
1925-1928
p. 46

AEROPLANE
HANGING LAMP
1925-1928   pp. 52-53

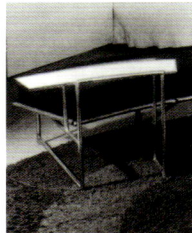

PORTABLE SIDE
TABLE 1928-1928
p. 45

SOFA BED
1925-1928
p. 49

JAPANESE-STYLE
LAMP 1925-1930
p. 42

E.1027 TABLE
1925-1930
p. 75

PORTABLE TABLE
1925-1930
p. 75

TRANSAT CHAIR
1925-1930
pp. 58-59

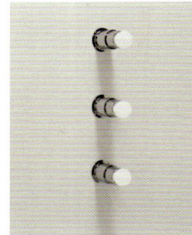

WALL LIGHTS
E.1027 HOUSE
1926-1928   p. 73

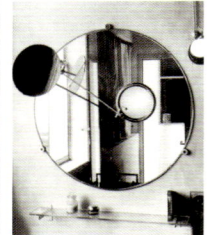

SATELLITE
MIRROR
p. 77

BLUE MARINE RUG
1926-1929
p. 66

CENTIMETER RUG
p. 67

WARDROBE
E.1027 HOUSE
1926-1929   p. 76

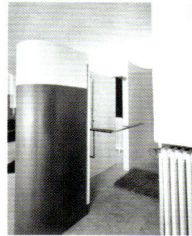

CURVED
CUPPBOARD E.1027
HOUSE 1926-1929

DRESSING CABINET
E.1027 HOUSE
1926-1929   p. 70

PERFORATED
SCREEN
1926-1929   p. 86

NON-CONFORMIST
CHAIR
1926-1929   pp. 62-63

CHAIR HOUSE E.1027
1926-1929
p. 63

CHEST WITH
PIVOTING DRAWERS
1926-1929

BATHROOM MIRROR
1926-1929
p. 72

DRESSING TABLE
E.1027 HOUSE
1925-1930   p. 77

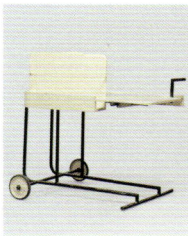

TROLLEY TABLE
E.1027 HOUSE
1926-1949   p. 79

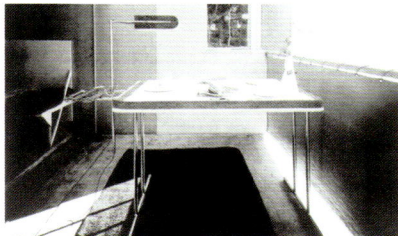

DINING TABLE E.1027 HOUSE
1926-1929
p. 65

E.1027 TABLE
1925-1930
p. 75

ADJUSTABLE
WRITING TABLE
E.1027 HOUSE
p. 68

FOLDING TEA TABLE HOUSE E.1027
1926-1929
p. 78

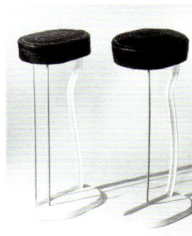

BAR STOOLS
E.1027 HOUSE
1926-1929   p. 112

DOUBLE X TABLE
1927-1929
pp. 80-81

SOFA BED WITH PIVOTING TABLE JEAN
BADOVICI APARTAMENT
p. 85

BATHROOM'S
METAL CURTAINS
1929-1931   p. 89

DESK WITH
ADJUSTABLE LIGHT
1929-1931   p. 84

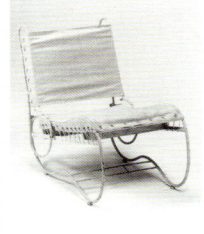

LOW OUTDOOR
ARMCHAIR 1930
p. 106

CHAIR
1930
p. 94

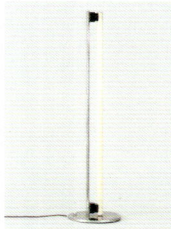

TUBULAR FLOOR
LAMP
pp. 90-91

CELLULOID
PERFORATED SCREEN
1931   p. 86

EXTENDING WARDROBE
1932-1934
p. 100

CUBIC DRAWER UNIT WITH PIVOTING
DRAWERS 1932-1934
p. 99

HEIGHT-
ADJUSTABLE TABLE
1932-1934   p. 103

DINING TABLE
1932-1934
p. 102

OUTDOOR TABLE
WITH TWO POSITIONS
1932-1934   p. 97

"SIÈGE COIFFEUSE"
CHAIR
1932-1934
p. 98

S-BEND CHAIR
1932-1934
pp. 110-111

OUTDOOR RECLINER
1935
pp. 108-109

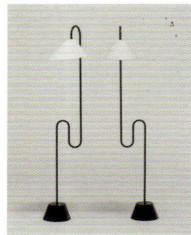

LAMP WITH
SWIVELING STAND
1935   p. 43

TABLE WITH WIRE
FRAME
1935   p. 104

TABLE WITH WIRE
FRAME
1935   p. 104

TABLE WITH WIRE
FRAME
1935   p. 104

BIBLIOGRAPHY

Peter Adam, *Eileen Gray. Her life and work*, London: Thames & Hudson, 2009.

Peter Adam, *Eileen Gray. Architect, designer: a biography*, London: Thames & Hudson, 2000.

Renaud Barres, Catherine Bernard, Caroline Constant, Oliver Gabet, Philippe Garner, Jennifer Goff, Anne Jacquin, Frederic Migayrou, Cloe Pitiot, Ruth Starr, et al. *Eileen Gray*, (Centre Pompidou, Paris) Pitiot, Cloe; Stritzler-Levine, Nina (eds.). New York: Bard Graduate Center, 2020.

François Baudot. *Eileen Gray*, London: Thames & Hudson, 1998.

Caroline Constant. *Eileen Gray*, Oxford: Phaidon, 2000.

Claudia Dona. «Il Razionalismo soft di una grande progettista», *Modo*, Italy, May 1980, pp. 45-49.

Carmen Espegel. *Proyecto E.1027 de Gray-Badovici. Drama de la villa moderna en el Mediterraneo*, Madrid: Escuela Politécnica de Madrid, Escuela Técnica Superior de Arquitectura, 1997.

Carmen Espegel. *Heroínas del espacio. Mujeres arquitectos en el movimiento moderno*, Valencia: Ediciones Generales de la Construcción, 2006.

Carmen Espegel. *Aires modernos. E.1027 maison en bord de mer: Eileen Gray y Jean Badovici, 1926-1929*, Madrid: Mairea Libros, 2010.

Philippe Garner. *Eileen Gray. Designer and Architect*, Cologne: Taschen, 1993.

Jennifer Goff (29 November 2013). *Eileen Gray: Her Work and Her World*. Newbridge, Irish Academic Press, 2013.

Eileen Gray. *E.1027. Maison en bord de mer*, Marseille: Imbernon, 2006.

Eileen Gray, Peter Adam, Andrew Lambirth. *Eileen Gray: the private painter*. London: Lund Humphries and Osborne Samuel, 2015.

Eileen Gray, et al. *Eileen Gray, An architecture for all senses*, Tübingen: Ernst J. Wasmuth, 1996.

Stefan Hecker and Christian Müller. *Eileen Gray, Works and projects*, Barcelona: Gustavo Gili, 1993.

Brigitte Loye, *Eileen Gray. 1879-1976. Architecture Design*, Paris: Editions Analeph/ J.P. Viguier, 1984.

Charlotte Malterre-Barthes and Zosia DzierĐawska. *Eileen Gray: A House Under the Sun*. London, Nobrow, 2019.

Luis Marín de Terán. «La visita de la vieja dama: Eileen Gray», *Arquitecturas Bis*, no. 16, Barcelona, November 1976, pp. 7-18.

Patricia O'Reilly. «Furniture as art: the work of Eileen Gray». *History Ireland*. Vol. 18 no. 3, 2010, pp. 42–46.

Jean-Paul Rayon. «Eileen Gray, un manifeste 1926-1929», *Architecture Mouvement Continuité*, Paris: November 1975, pp. 49-56.

Jean-Paul Rayon and Brigitte Loye. «Eileen Gray architetto, 1879-1976», *Casabella*, no. 480, Milan: 1982, pp. 38-45.

Penelope Rowlands. *Eileen Gray*, San Francisco: Chronicle, 2002.

Penelope Rowlands, Marisa Bartolucci, Eileen Gray (eds.). *Eileen Gray*. San Francisco, Chronicle Books, 2002.

Joseph Rykwert. «Un Omaggio a Eileen Gray: pioniera del design», *Domus*, no. 469, Milan: December 1968, pp. 21-34.

Joseph Rykwert. «Eileen Gray: two houses and an interior, 1926-1933», *Perspecta*, 13-14, Yale: 1971, pp. 66-73.

Joseph Rykwert. "Eileen Gray: pioneer of design", *Architectural Review Vol. CLII*, no. 910, London: December 1972, pp. 357-361.

Pedro Sambrano (2015). *Eileen Gray: her work and her world*. Newbridge, Irish Academic Press., 2015.